THE FOUR ELEMENTS OF SUCCESSFUL MANAGEMENT

THE FOUR
ELEMENTS OF
SUCCESSFUL
MANAGEMENT

Select • Direct
Evaluate • Reward

Don R. Marshall

AMACOM
American Management Association
New York • Atlanta • Boston • Chicago • Kansas City • San Francisco • Washington, D. C.
Brussels • Mexico City • Tokyo • Toronto

Library of Congress Cataloging-in-Publication Data

Marshall, Don R., 1939–
        The four elements of successful management / Don R. Marshall.
                p.   cm.
        Includes index.
        ISBN 0-8144-0424-3
        1. Management.   I. Title.
    HD30.3.M36669   1998
        658—dc21   98-29548
                                                                          CIP

Printing number

10   9   8   7   6   5   4   3   2   1

*To Carol.
And to Rick and Chris,
the results of her successful management skills.*

Contents

Preface   xiii

Part One   **SELECT**   **1**

Chapter 1   **Defining the Job**   **3**
               Determining Job Responsibilities   4
               Conducting a Job Audit   7
               Sidebar: Replacing an Employee   *8*
               Drafting a Job Description   9
               Sidebar: Structure vs. Creativity: A Red
               Herring   *10*
               Determining Salary Range   13

Chapter 2   **Finding Qualified Candidates**   **15**
               Who Are the Candidates?   16
               Ideal-Candidate Profile   16
               Where Are the Candidates?   17
               Internal vs. External Candidates   17
               Employed vs. Unemployed
               Candidates   18
               Sidebar: Relocation Issues   *19*
               How Can You Inform the Candidates
               and Interest Them in the Position?   20
               The "Reach-In" Process   21
               Newspaper Advertising   22
               Search/Employment Firms and
               Services   23
               Internet Advertising and Résumé
               Search Services   24

	Trade and Professional Associations and Publications	24
	Alumni Associations and School Bulletin Boards	25
	Radio and Cable Television Advertising	25
	Networking	26
	Outplacement Firms	26
	Temporary Employment Agencies	26
	How Many Candidates Are Enough?	27
Chapter 3	**Filling the Job**	**28**
	Using Résumés to Screen Candidates	29
	Interviewing Candidates by Telephone	30
	Interviewing Candidates Face-to-Face	32
	Sidebar: Evaluating Work-Related Attitude and Drive	*33*
	Structure Your Interviews With Objectives and an Outline	34
	Stick to Your Outline	35
	Get Past the "Stranger" Stage	36
	Use Your Time Wisely	36
	Talk Less and Listen More!	36
	Sidebar: Assessing Communication Skills: The 3-by-5 Card Test	*37*
	Don't Overrely on Intuition	38
	Sidebar: Preemployment Testing	*38*
	Avoid the Stress Interview and the "Group Grope"	39
	Checking References	40
	Making the Offer	41
	The Offer Letter	43
	What If They're Not Out There?	44
Part Two	**DIRECT**	**45**
Chapter 4	**Determining Direction**	**47**
	Why Direction Is Important	49

	Why Managers Don't Give Proper Direction	52
	Sidebar: A Few Words About Goals and Process	*54*
	Can There Be Too Much Direction?	55
	Determining What to Direct	56
	Management: A Top-Down Affair	59
Chapter 5	**Training Management in Direction**	**62**
	Why Training Is Necessary	63
	Sidebar: Training—Consider Renaming It	*65*
	Training for Managers	66
	Phase 1. Translation of Company Objectives	68
	Stage 1. Translate Company Objectives Into Action Steps With Deadlines	68
	Stage 2. Break Down Major Action Steps Into Specific Substeps	69
	Stage 3. Assign Substeps to Functions, With Deadlines	70
	Phase 2. Training in Assigning Action Steps	74
	Section VIII. Where Managers Learn the Basics of Direction	77
	Direction and the Job Audit	81
	Objectives: Ceilings or Minimums?	83
	Sidebar: Leave Time for Local Objectives	*83*
Chapter 6	**Training Nonmanagement Personnel**	**85**
	Positioning the Training Program	86
	Phase 1. Sharing the Strategic Plan With Employees	89
	Phase 2. Receiving and Performing Action-Step Assignments	92
	Implementing Phase 2	95
	Who Conducts These Sessions and How?	96
	Measuring Progress	97

Part Three   Evaluate   **99**

Chapter 7   **Knowing What to Evaluate**   **101**

Why Measuring Performance Is
     Important   103

     The Sheriff-and-Posse Strategy   104

Handling Behavioral Issues as They
     Arise   106

Developing Employee-Driven
     Evaluations   108

Evaluation: The Manager's Report
     Card   116

Chapter 8   **The Evaluation Meeting**   **118**

Why Managers Hate Evaluation   118

Collecting Better Input Data   121

     Critical Incidents File   122

     Objectives and Action Steps   122

     Performance Evaluation Forms   123

     Job Descriptions   123

     Compensation Changes   123

     Employee Preparation   124

     Input for Management Employees   125

     Avoiding Confrontation   126

Creating Greater Confidence in the
     Process   127

Conducting More-Productive Meetings   129

     Sidebar: Three Rules for Productive
         Evaluation Meetings   *132*

Improving Personnel Utilization in the
     Future   132

Chapter 9   **Using Evaluations**   **134**

How Evaluations Should Be Used   134

How Evaluations Should *Not* Be Used   135

Performance Categories and How to
     Handle Them   137

     Handling Employees Who Deserve
         Immediate or Eventual Promotion   139

     Handling Promotions to Management-
         Level Positions   141

Handling Employees With
  Questionable Promotion Potential 143
Handling Employees in the Possible-
  Retention Subcategory 145
Handling Employees Who Are Not
  Retainable 146
Using a Management Review Board to
  Ensure Consistent Evaluations 147

Part Four **REWARD** **149**

Chapter 10 **The Purpose of Rewards** **151**
Rewards: An Integral Part of Selection 152
Focusing on Time and Cost When
  Rewarding Employees 154
Developing and Installing a Base-Pay
  System 156
Merit Pay or Automatic Rewards:
  Which Is More Appropriate? 160
How Merit and Automatic Progression
  Programs Affect Employee Groups 161
Rewarding Performance With Merit
  and Automatic Progression
  Programs 163
Performance Evaluation and Merit or
  Automatic Progression Programs 164
Pay Grade Ranges and Merit vs.
  Automatic Increases 164
Withholding Rewards 165

Chapter 11 **Variable-Reward and Nonpay-
  Reward Programs** **167**
Why Managers Don't Like Variable
  Rewards 168
Using Variable Rewards to
  Acknowledge Group and Individual
  Efforts 169
Using Variable Rewards to Increase
  Quality 170

Selecting and Installing a Variable-
　　Reward Program 172
　　　Management Bonuses 173
　　　Commissions to Salespeople 175
　　　Gain Sharing 176
　　　Skill-Based Pay 178
Using Nonpay Rewards 179
Key Ingredients of Variable-Reward
　　Programs: Time and Energy 181

Chapter 12　Administering a Reward Program **183**
Management Training: A Must for Any
　　Reward System 183
Communicating the Program to
　　Employees 184
Administering the Program 185
Evaluating Pay and Creating Pay
　　Ranges 187
Adjusting Pay Ranges and
　　Administering Pay Increases 189
　　　General Increases 190
　　　COLA Increases 191
　　　Promotion Rewards 192
Using Exceptional Rewards 193
　　　Red-Circle Reward Levels 193
　　　Lump-Sum Rewards 194
　　　Exempt Overtime 194

Afterword: Go Forth and Manage! 197

Index 201

Preface

Someone once wrote, "To some people life is a dance, to others it is a wrestling match, to the rest it is a jail term."

People who feel life is a dance never get themselves into management jobs. They spend their time twirling and waving their arms in the air in time to life's music. They don't want to be responsible for others. To them, life is to be enjoyed, not burdened with management-type duties. Besides, nobody would ask them to be managers anyway.

Those who feel life is a jail term also never become managers. Their basically negative outlook on almost everything prevents them from being promoted to or striving for a management job. They may supervise others in their own small business, but they most likely have never been and never would be selected by someone else to be a manager.

That brings us to people who see life as a wrestling match. If you're in a management position, this is your group—the group for whom this book is written.

Some people are born wrestlers, but the average person has to be trained in basic wrestling skills. There's no accurate way to tell if someone is a born wrestler, so everyone who wants to be a wrestler needs to learn the basic holds. The same is true for managers. It doesn't matter whether they are born or developed over time. What is important is that they identify and develop the skills they need. Sometimes managers recognize these skills early in their management career; other times, a moment of enlightenment suddenly illuminates the fundamentals and they become almost second nature.

Education is incremental. Enlightenment is not. If you ignore the incremental process of learning, you are depending on enlightenment. You are hoping that you or someone else will eventually find the way. That's not likely to happen, and it isn't good business management.

Businesses compete—and so do their managers. The businesses with the better managers almost always come out on top. The nonmanagement employees of businesses also compete, because they have a considerable effect on the costs of their business's operation. If an employee fails to perform or performs marginally, you don't get your money back; yet many managers deal with less than required performance as if it were a lamp from Sears—returnable with a full refund!

The purpose of management is to accomplish objectives as quickly as possible at the lowest costs. But because goals and objectives constantly shift and exact cost accounting is impossible or impractical, achieving goals is not easy. Many times managers find themselves hoping that the outcome will meet the goals, rather than really managing the events and the people.

When things don't go as expected, many managers ask, "What's wrong with these people working for me?" The question should be, "What's wrong with the way I'm managing these people who are working for me?" Everything that goes wrong in the business is management's fault! If it is seen as not being management's fault, than management has relinquished its control in that situation. It is always management's fault!

If the business, or department, is not reaching its goals or objectives, the first question a manager should ask is, "Am I hiring the correct people?" If the correct people are being hired, the next question should be, "Am I directing them correctly?" If direction is sufficient, the next question to ask is, "Am I evaluating their performance correctly?" The last aspect to look at is, "Am I rewarding the employees correctly?"

Each of those questions focuses on one of the four basic elements of management, which I call Select, Direct, Evaluate, and Reward. Those four elements form the framework of all people and performance management. They are the equivalent of wrestling's basic holds. They are what often comes out of that moment of enlightenment. They are what some managers already know to be the fundamental elements of management, and every other manager should learn.

People tend to make things more complicated than they are by paying too much attention to details. It's better to identify the framework or skeleton that supports a body of work. Life functions around various sets of basic elements. We need to eat, drink, and sleep in order to keep our bodies functioning. All of our awareness as humans is based on the use of sight, hearing, smell, taste, and touch. Our basic physical orientation at any time is either running, walking, standing, sitting, or lying down. It is the identification of elements that are common to an area of performance that allows for quick achievement of results in that endeavor.

Likewise, the framework of management is built upon selection, direction, evaluation, and reward. Once these elements are understood, managers—whether new or seasoned—can develop their own style around this framework. This structure and framework is the "big picture" of management. Each element is vital. Overlooking any one of these ingredients will dramatically affect the effectiveness of an organization.

Management trends and fads will come and go, but the selection, direction, evaluation, and reward of people will always be critical to all management responsibility. Techniques within each of the elements may improve or simply change, but failure to administer any one or more of the four professionally will result in inferior management performance. Effectively applying all four elements leads to positive results.

This book provides the incremental lessons in understanding and applying those basic elements, or what I call the Four Elements of Successful Management. The book is directed primarily to entry-level and mid-level managers. In my experience as an operations manager and management consultant, I've found that these managers often don't have real insights into the hard-nosed aspects of running a business. They focus on feelings instead of results. They manage people instead of tasks. They are not certain how to find their bearings in markets that change constantly and companies that try to respond. And in a world bursting with management theories, they're not sure which ones to embrace.

It's my belief that when managers understand the Four Elements of Successful Management, they can better focus their efforts and, as a result, do a better job of carrying out their core responsibilities. This produces quicker results and makes them capable of increasing their effectiveness within the company and furthering their management careers.

In management, as in any endeavor, basic skills must be developed before exceptional performance can be achieved. The wrestler works at developing and maintaining basic holds and moves because, when perfected, they provide the means to deal with the majority of the challenges to be faced. Not doing this will place any wrestler at a real disadvantage against world-class competitors who have mastered these basic elements. Likewise, the manager who develops and polishes these four basic elements will be prepared to match wits and staff against any contender.

PART ONE

Select

Whenever I ask managers which of the Four Elements of Successful Management—Select, Direct, Evaluate, or Reward—they spend the most time on, they always answer, "Directing." When I ask which element is the most important, they always answer, "Selection."

In my opinion, the reason managers spend so much time directing is that they do a poor job on selection. Instead of filling jobs, they simply hire people; instead of taking the time to identify and prioritize job tasks and responsibilities, they develop a rough sketch of a "qualified person" and force-fit a match.

Part One will give you the tools you need to avoid making these mistakes and to select employees who have the talents, attitude, background, and motivation to succeed in the job you have in mind. It will help you to:

- ❑ Define clearly the job you hope to fill.
- ❑ Set performance standards.
- ❑ Create a profile of your ideal candidate.
- ❑ Advertise for candidates and interview them effectively.

Follow these steps and you will greatly increase the likelihood of crafting a lasting match between a viable job and a qualified candidate. Neglect them and you'll pay for indifferently selected candidates again and again.

CHAPTER 1

Defining the Job

In my opinion, the Apollo moon mission was the greatest management exercise in the history of the world. The great pyramids may have been an engineering marvel, but getting them built was a matter of managing thousands of bodies, paying no wages, and never publishing a body count. Likewise, the Panama Canal could have been built no matter what obstacles presented themselves by simply adding more people, time, and money. But the Apollo moon mission was something different.

Managers had built pyramids and canals before—but no one had ever sent men to the moon and brought them back alive. Even ancient explorers like Columbus, although traveling to unexplored or unknown places, could almost always rely on ocean currents to eventually reach land should their power source, the wind in their sails, fail them. They just weren't sure where that land was located. Power-source failure in the Apollo mission, on the other hand, had a much more hazardous potential. It could mean crashing during takeoff, or disappearing into the far reaches of space with the oxygen supply quickly running out, or orbiting the moon in decreasing altitudes until a crash into its surface ended the mission.

The people managing the Apollo project faced an extremely difficult staffing problem. They couldn't advertise for engineers or astronauts with "manned lunar landing and retrieval experience." They couldn't just hire capable people and train them, because no one was sure what skills the project would demand. The first problem was not how to *find* the right people. It was how to *define* the right jobs.

Before they hired anyone, the mission managers convened

a group of experts with education, experience, or exposure to space engineering or flight and assigned them the task of determining the jobs to be performed in order to accomplish the clearly defined objective of the group's customer, the U.S. government.

What was true for the Apollo moon mission is true for managers today: Before you can select the best people for a job, you need to know what job has to be performed. Unless a job is carefully defined up front, there is no way to judge whether the right person has been selected.

That is why the first step in the selection process is to *define the job*. This sounds like a logical step, but in my experience, many managers launch the search process without performing it. Not until mid-search do they realize that they aren't clear about what they want from the job *or* the candidate, and then they continue on anyway. This can spell disaster for a company and doom the match between job and hire.

The only way to ensure a successful selection process is to define the job first. Once its responsibilities and tasks have been defined, it can be designed to meet and fulfill the customer's expectations and create the results your organization wants.

There are four steps involved in defining a job:

1. Determining job responsibilities
2. Conducting a job audit
3. Drafting a job description
4. Determining salary range

Let's look at these one by one.

Determining Job Responsibilities

Before you begin the candidate search process, take time to compile a list of job responsibilities and tasks that the potential new hire will be doing during the first one or two years of employment (see Exhibit 1-1). Rank specific tasks from most to least important, most to least difficult, or most to least time-consum-

Exhibit 1-1. List of the projected responsibilities and tasks of the position to be filled.

Position Responsibilities and Tasks

Position title: Manager, Quality Control
Reports to: Manager, Operations
Date: xx/xx/xx

General Responsibilities

Develop and manage programs and procedures designed to continually improve product quality while reducing quality-related costs.

Specific Tasks

1. Prepare organization for ISO 9000 certification.

2. Develop and install effective quality cost model.

3. Achieve the following short-term objectives:

    a. Reduce reject rate by 50 percent over next three months.

    b. Establish three effective continuous improvement teams within three months.

    c. Complete quality documentation program within six months.

Completed by: _____

---

ing. To be as specific and descriptive as possible, use action words like those listed in Exhibit 1-2.

Pass the list around to the internal customers of the potential new hire—i.e., other managers who have related responsibilities or who depend on services to be provided by the new person. Feedback from these customers will help you determine whether the job as described will meet their needs. Even if you, as hiring manager, are the only person who fully understands the need for the new employee, you should still take the time to gather feedback in order to reinforce your convictions.

Exhibit 1-2. Action words for writing job responsibilities.

accounts for	directs	maintains	reworks
acts	discovers	makes	reviews
adjusts	drafts	manipulates	
analyzes	drives	matches	schedules
answers		mixes	secures
applies	estimates		selects
approves	examines	observes	sells
arranges	figures	obtains	sets
assigns	files	operates	shapes
assists	finds	orders	signs
	follows	organizes	sketches
cares for	formulates		stamps
carries		performs	standardizes
checks	gauges	places	stores
cleans up		plans	supervises
closes	handles	prepares	systematizes
compares	inspects	processes	
composes	installs	proposes	takes
computes	instructs	pulls	teaches
conducts	interprets		totals
constructs	investigates	ranks	types
controls	issues	reads	
coordinates	itemizes	receives	uses
		recognizes	utilizes
decides	judges	records	verifies
designates		refers	voids
designs	keeps	removes	
details	lays out	repairs	writes
determines	lifts	requests	

Once managers agree that this list of responsibilities and tasks fills a legitimate company need requiring the investment in a full-time, permanent hire, you will know that a job indeed needs to be filled. If the other managers do not agree with you, find out what they want instead. You may want to rethink the job based on their feedback.

Several benefits are derived from this process:

❑ A careful assessment of a job's potential responsibilities may reveal that those duties are already being performed by someone else or no longer have to be performed at all. If you find this out *before* you hire someone, you'll save money. If you discover it *after* someone is hired, you'll have a bored employee on your hands—not to mention additional payroll, benefits, space, equipment, and administrative costs.

❑ Defining responsibilities makes it harder to hire a "personality" and then look for a job the person can do—an expensive but common move. Too many managers believe that they can always find something for a good person to do or someone a good person can replace. When managers hire people instead of fill jobs, sales-per-employee numbers begin to deteriorate and owners or company presidents start to question poor productivity figures. Hiring a person is not the same as filling a job!

❑ It will help create a flawless match between candidate and responsibility. Candidates tend to believe that they are being hired to do what their résumé says they do well. Once hired, they can be disappointed if they find out that the position's priorities aren't what they thought they were and don't even interest them. If you take the time to pinpoint the job's responsibilities, applicants can clearly and honestly assess whether they are interested in meeting these responsibilities.

Conducting a Job Audit

When an overworked department begs you for some help, what's a manager to do? Too many managers respond by hiring more people. A better approach is to examine how the tasks that

---

Replacing an Employee

When someone leaves the company or is promoted, you need to hire a replacement, right? Wrong. When someone is terminated for failure to perform, the required job duties are apparent because they were not being performed. But someone who leaves voluntarily may not have been challenged because his or her job lacked substance. If that was the case, there won't be much for a successor to do, either.

Don't fill any position, new or existing, until you have conducted an audit of its responsibilities. Write a new job definition and circulate the list of responsibilities and tasks among internal customers to justify the position. You may discover that the position doesn't have to be filled because responsibilities can be redistributed—or that the job wasn't much of a job after all!

---

need to be done fit with overall department work patterns. This approach, called a job audit, helps eliminate tasks that, over time, have accumulated within jobs—tasks that people continue to do well even though they may no longer be necessary to the job or the company. A job audit may reveal that no new help is needed at all—that the backlog can be eased by changing the work process or redistributing the work in a department.

To audit the jobs in your department, gather a team to develop a flowchart of its work. Have the team break the department's work into discrete steps and then examine the rationale behind each one. Prepare yourself for surprises. In one company I worked with, all work orders had to go to the company president's secretary before they could be released. No one could explain why this had to happen; it just did. Eventually I discovered that five years earlier, the president had taken an extended European vacation. During his absence, he asked his secretary to collect work orders so that he could monitor the business through daily phone calls. Five years later, the secretary was still collecting work orders even though the president never looked at them.

Jobs change along with methods, technology, schedules, competition, and customer requirements. That is why all organizations should audit job content annually. More frequent audits are a good idea for companies that are growing quickly, developing new work processes, or adding or changing products and services. No job stays the same as a company grows. A careful audit will identify tasks that are obsolete and help managers redesign work processes to meet new goals and objectives.

Without an audit, a company or department head may assume that current employees are following the correct procedures and focusing on the right tasks. But people tend to accommodate their own weaknesses, prejudices, strengths, capabilities, opinions, fears, and goals—with results that may differ from tasks and procedures that are efficient, customer-driven, and beneficial for the company and its employees.

If your company doesn't have an ongoing job audit process, take the initiative and establish one to review employees' activities. Every activity, every movement, every task that goes into a job has both a cost and a benefit to the company. An annual job audit will help reveal whether a job's benefit outweighs its cost—so that if it doesn't, you can redesign the position to make it more efficient.

After all, the purpose of any business is to convert its assets and resources, including human resources, into a profit. Too many organizations wait until they're in financial trouble to pinpoint and eliminate unnecessary activities. People often can't find the time to maintain something, but they always find the time to fix it! Avoid this mistake by making a regular job audit process part of your ongoing responsibilities.

Drafting a Job Description

Many organizations change too quickly to write formal job descriptions. Others feel that formal job descriptions are . . . well, simply too formal. But a job description is an essential, living document that changes with the job and the company.

A formal job description serves several purposes. Because it describes duties and responsibilities, a job description sets the

Structure vs. Creativity: A Red Herring

Some managers—especially in companies where structure has a bad reputation—shy away from defining jobs, auditing the work process, and writing detailed job descriptions because they believe doing those things will create too much structure. There are companies, particularly smaller ones, that are prone to believing that structure is evil, that it strangles creativity and imposes needless layers of administration. These companies feel that their growth comes from giving people the freedom to react to situations, and that to structure organizational practices would only curtail this freedom. They fear that adding to or changing the structure would unravel their success.

But that's just not so. When small companies succeed, it is because key people know just what to do to move the company forward in a cost-effective manner. They identify important tasks or problems and then benefit from measuring the company's success in performing those tasks or solving those problems. Structure is simply a matter of translating this task-oriented, measurement-based focus from an individual to an organization. It's a matter of designing tasks so that people know where and how to spend their energy.

Without structure, it would be pointless—not to mention expensive—to gather fifty people in a room and tell them, "Process insurance claims." Imagine the redundant work and the overlooked tasks! But gather them into a room and give them formal job descriptions and a reporting structure, and those insurance claims will be processed quickly and cost-effectively.

Both organizations and people need skeletons in order to provide strength for growth—and for organizations, structure is that skeleton. The bigger the organization, the bigger its skeletal structure. But structure doesn't mean rigidity or immobility.

Structured companies with internal policies and procedures that ensure consistency often succeed because they know what to do and how to do it. They also know what *not* to do. This kind of structure ensures consistent quality and service to customers as well as consistent company results.

> Consistency in itself is not the objective. Identifying the correct tasks and procedures and then ensuring their consistent application is the goal. Think of consistency as a fire drill that you practice over and over so that you can get out of the building as quickly and efficiently as possible. Once you know the quickest and shortest way to the door, you'll want to establish that route as the standard procedure.

salary for the position—and you need to establish a salary range before you can attract candidates. And because it establishes standards for accomplishing tasks, a job description can serve as a performance evaluation tool. If excessive management is required to get a certain employee to perform required tasks, you'll know that the wrong person has been selected to fill that job.

A job description also facilitates the annual job-audit process. Formal descriptions offer a quick summary of company or department responsibilities and make it easier to determine whether the tasks you are paying for are essential in accomplishing company or department objectives.

An assembly-line job is easy to describe because its tasks are easy to identify and are generally designed into the manufacturing process. At higher levels in the organization, tasks and responsibilities are harder to define. Still, it is essential to write a description with clearly defined and measurable tasks, such as "meet the needs of an ever increasing customer base while maintaining or increasing margins." No matter what level of job you are trying to fill, identifying its tasks and responsibilities is absolutely essential.

State every job's tasks and objectives in measurable terms, such as quantity, quality, and time. After all, the basis of business is measurement. To create a job that, when it is described, does not include measurable elements is to ignore performance standards. We tend to think that standards of performance come into play only when it's time to evaluate employees, but they also play a key role in selecting new hires.

Selecting employees is the same as selecting tools for any type of project. The tools you select determine how long it takes to produce a product, how many will be produced, and the quality of the product or service once the process is completed. Most companies compete on the basis of delivery time, quality, and cost. Whether they can do something is not as important as whether they can do it faster, better, and more efficiently than the competition.

Suppose a prize of $1,000,000 were offered to anyone who could memorize a page from the dictionary. Any reader who took the time to attack the problem would qualify to win. But offering the prize to the first five people to memorize the page would considerably narrow the field of contenders. Likewise, the urgency of a specific job should be considered along with the competence of the candidate. Just because someone can eventually do the job does not mean that he or she will do it in the required time frame.

Thus, every job description should include standards of performance that clearly define success and failure on the job. An easy way to determine standards for a position is to list issues that would cause someone to be fired. Failure to perform what tasks by what deadline and in what manner would result in termination? Working backward will prevent you from writing vague, unmeasurable standards.

Every manager and employee should be in complete agreement on the most important elements and goals for that employee's job. Establishing and communicating a precise job description and clear standards is your job as a manager. Any manager who neglects to clarify and communicate job responsibilities and standards—who says things like, "I'm not sure Bob is getting the job done; he's not working on the things I consider important. I'll have to get around to talking to him about this"—is simply not managing.

If the selection element is the most important of Select, Direct, Evaluate, and Reward, then clearly describing the job's content and standards of performance is the most important element of the selection process. Without a clearly defined job and a formal job description, you cannot find and hire the correct candidate.

Determining Salary Range

Responsibilities and salary are always related. Once you have drawn up a list of job duties and responsibilities and have written a job description, determining a corresponding salary range should be easy—especially if your company uses a formal program to evaluate jobs and determine pay grades within the company.

Roughly speaking, all jobs can be sorted into three categories:

1. *Nonexempt jobs* are those that involve performing prescribed, internal tasks and include little problem solving. Federal regulations require that workers in this category be paid time and a half for overtime hours. (They are "nonexempt" from these regulations.) These jobs are at the lower end of the pay-grade structure.

2. *Exempt jobs* are those associated with supervising the performance of internal tasks and dealing with problems related to those tasks. These employees do not need to be paid overtime for extra hours. A good rule of thumb for determining whether a job is exempt is this: If you miss a day of work and someone else does your work for you during your absence, your job is probably nonexempt. But if you return to work and find your work waiting for you, you're probably exempt.

3. *Management positions* are those involving responsibility for addressing internal and external problems and programs, such as business objectives and challenges.

Avoid the temptation to inflate a job's title by pasting the management label on a task-based job. People with management skills cost more money in the job market and are harder to hire. Let's say you decide to speed up your company's inefficient employee health-care claims handling process by creating a new position: someone who will collect claim forms and coordinate with your insurance carrier. Don't lose sight of the fact that you are hiring someone to perform a series of tasks, not to address a management problem. Advertise for a clerk or a coordinator, not a manager.

Always establish the correct responsibility level and salary range for every opening you advertise. Doing so will provide consistency throughout your department and maintain internal equity in the structuring and compensation of jobs.

CHAPTER 2

Finding Qualified Candidates

The goal of the search process is never just to fill a job. Filling a job is easy. What makes the search process hard is making sure you meet your objective: to hire a person who will return a significant value to the organization over the short and long term.

In order to find someone who will return a significant value to the organization, you need to find viable candidates. A candidate is not someone who is interested in the job; it is someone who, at least on the surface, is qualified to be seriously considered for the job.

To find a viable group of candidates, you need to answer four questions:

1. Who are the candidates?
2. Where are the candidates?
3. How can you inform the candidates of and interest them in the position?
4. How many candidates are enough?

Answering these questions will help you find applicants who can seriously be considered as candidates. So will drafting a clear and detailed job description. You need to know exactly what you're looking for to determine where to cast your net and when to stop casting. By defining the job and the candidate, you'll increase your chances of finding a great candidate and crafting a profitable, long-lasting match.

Who Are the Candidates?

Ideal-Candidate Profile

You don't have the time or the resources to evaluate every appli-
cant who strolls in. To guide your work, you should develop a
profile of your "ideal" candidate. You may never find your ideal,
but you will establish a basic framework that outlines the person
you are looking for.

Developing an ideal candidate profile is similar to viewing
a lineup of suspects after you've witnessed a bank robbery. The
individual you pick out may not be the actual bank robber, but
chances are the real criminal is strongly similar. Often, a lineup
helps police establish the silhouette or basic framework of the
person being sought. The profile is clear even if the details are
not. Likewise, your ideal-candidate profile will give you a
sharper idea of what you are really looking for, so that you can
increase your odds of finding him or her.

Use the following outline to develop a profile of your ideal
candidate:

1. *Must* have, or have done, or be able to do:
    a. Experience: type and years
    b. Industry: type, or specific companies, and years
    c. Skills or talents
    d. Education
2. *Should* have, or have done, or be able to do:
    a. Experience: type and years
    b. Industry: type, or specific companies, and years
    c. Skills or talents
    d. Education
3. *Would be nice* to have, or have done, or be able to do:
    a. Experience: type and years
    b. Industry: type, or specific companies, and years
    c. Skills or talents
    d. Education

Be specific when you draft your outline. If you want someone with strong follow-up skills, say so. If you want an assertive

person who can handle high stress, say so. To create a good match between job and candidate, you need to define the person as closely as you define the job.

Keep your company culture in mind, too. If your company is team-oriented and flexible, you want a candidate who is comfortable with teamwork—and not everyone is. If your department is highly structured, you want someone who works well in a structured situation. Describe the qualities that your company values so that you can find compatible candidates.

Just remember that defining the candidate is a lot like shopping for groceries: The more you toss into your shopping cart, the more you'll pay. The cost of filling a job is influenced by two factors: how long it takes to find the candidate, and the supply of qualified candidates. The greater the number of *must have* items on your list, the longer it's going to take to find that person. The greater the experience, skills, or education requirements, the smaller the supply of candidates and the larger the compensation package required to hire the person.

Where Are the Candidates?

As a rule candidates for a given position are available both inside (i.e., internal candidates) and outside (i.e., external candidates) your company. Internal candidates already work in your department or another department in your company. External candidates work for your direct competitors or for companies in another field or industry.

Internal vs. External Candidates

For a number of reasons, internal candidates are often best. First, filling a job from within is almost always less costly, because it takes less time to locate, interview, and commit to someone in your company or department—and time is money when it comes to filling jobs. Second, an internal candidate is a known quantity in terms of experience, attitude, work practices, ability, and, to a degree, potential. Third, an internal promotion generally triggers other internal promotions. If you promote employee A into the open job, employee B into A's vacated job, employee C into B's job, and so on, eventually the opening to be filled from outside will be an entry-level job—far easier and cheaper to fill.

The fourth and best reason for promoting from within is that you will pay less than the market rate for the job you're trying to fill, even when a raise is factored in. If you try to hire an outsider with a similar position, you will have to add to that person's market wage rate to persuade him or her to join your company. Even when a candidate's experience and expertise justify paying an above-market salary, you won't be as certain of his or her personal characteristics and ability to fit into your organization's culture.

In my opinion, you can't lose with an internal candidate. If the person doesn't work out, you can redefine his or her responsibilities or set up a transfer to another department. But it's hard to "dehire" an outsider whose attitude, values, or skills simply don't work or don't fit the company. You'll have more room to maneuver with an internal candidate. That's why the best place to start seeking candidates is in your own department. Extend your search to other departments if no qualified candidates are on your staff. If your search leaves you empty-handed, you'll need to look outside.

Lack of internal talent isn't the only reason to go outside your company. You may need an infusion of new blood and new ideas, or have a new position requiring new skills. Again, a clear job description and an understanding of the job's objective can help you decide whether to step up your search internally or go outside. When you do begin to look outside, the job description can help you know where to look. You won't know where to look until you know what you are looking for!

Employed vs. Unemployed Candidates

In my opinion, whether a candidate is employed or out of work is immaterial.

People who look for jobs while they're still working share certain traits. They are ambitious, because they want more than they have. They are action-oriented, because they are prepared

Relocation Issues

Whenever you go outside your organization to fill a position, you face the possibility of having to pay to relocate someone. The more remote your facility, the more likely it is that you will need to relocate a new employee. If there are no similar operations within 100 miles—say, you're in rural Nevada, or yours is the only tool and die maker for miles around—you will probably need to cover the new employee's housing relocation costs. Likewise, the more unique the job is in your organization, the more likely it is that someone will need to relocate. You may be able to promote a first-line supervisor from within, but there may not be a suitable internal candidate for vice president of operations.

Because the costs are similar whether you relocate a family a hundred miles or a thousand, don't limit your search for candidates to a particular area. Remember, your objective is not simply to fill the job, but to place in the job a person who will return a significant value to the organization over the short and long term. If the best candidate is a thousand miles away, recruitment and relocation costs matter little compared to the alternative of hiring a less qualified candidate who lives closer. In fact, someone who relocates farther is more likely to make a commitment to your organization and less likely to consider moving on soon.

Some families relocate eagerly, others reluctantly. Some family members are pleasantly surprised when they arrive; others see their worst fears come to pass. Your company can do everything possible to help in the relocation—provide information on schools and community activities, even help the spouse find a suitable job—but when the Welcome Wagon leaves and the front door closes, it's up to that family to make the move work. While the company has little control over the relocated family's adjustment, it has considerable control over ensuring a solid match of job and new hire. The better the new hire feels about his or her new job, the greater the chances that the entire experience will be a successful one for all involved.

to do something about their situation. They are somewhat impatient with slow progress, because they don't want to wait for things to change through someone else's efforts. They have the confidence to push things in their jobs, because they know that if they find themselves out of work, they will always find something else.

On the other hand, people who are out of work are not necessarily poor performers. There are plenty of poor performers who are working; they just haven't been caught yet! Plenty of people find themselves out of work through company reorganizations, downsizings, and other circumstances beyond their control. Most of them know that they will be valuable to some other employer once they find a good match.

How Can You Inform the Candidates and Interest Them in the Position?

There are several search methods you can use to spread the word about a job outside your organization and develop a candidate pool:

1. The "reach-in" process
2. Newspaper advertising
3. Search/employment firms and services
4. Internet advertising and résumé search services
5. Trade and professional associations and publications
6. Alumni associations and school bulletin boards
7. Radio and cable television advertising
8. Networking
9. Outplacement firms
10. Temporary employment agencies

Let's take a brief look at each one. (For more detailed information on recruitment methods, see Diane Arthur, *Recruiting, Interviewing, Selecting and Orienting New Employees*, 3d ed. [New York: AMACOM, 1998].)

The "Reach-In" Process

To find external candidates, many managers run an advertisement in a newspaper or trade journal. But your best source of good external candidates is companies that your company competes with for similar types of jobs, or even in terms of products or services. To contact these people, you "reach in" to the other company through a letter or phone call placed on your behalf by a third party, such as a recruiter or a search firm. Don't do this yourself! The reach-in strategy is always risky, but working with a third party is less so. A third party will get better results, and you won't gain a reputation for pirating people from within a common industry or face legal action for placing the call yourself.

A business intelligence company can help you find the names and addresses of specific people who work for your direct competitors or for companies that compete for the same sections of the labor market. The recruiter will use these to send each person a letter on its stationery that says, in brief, "I represent a client who is looking for someone with a background in _____ who would be interested in filling the position of _____. If you or anybody you know might be interested, call me for details." If the pool of potential candidates is less than a dozen or so, the search firm may contact them by phone. Once three or four candidates have been identified, the recruiter passes along résumés and summaries of any meetings or conversations, and you start interviewing.

Some people believe that persuading people to leave a current employer for your company is unethical. But running an ad seeks the same results. The only difference is that while almost everyone responding to a newspaper ad is interested in making a change, the majority of people contacted by reaching in are not. Also, the recruiter making the call on your behalf is simply presenting an opportunity, not trying to convince the candidate to take the job. In a tight labor market, reaching in is a very cost-effective way to fish where the fish are already swimming. Whether they bite depends upon the presentation and the product or opportunity, and on whether or not they are hungry.

Only when candidates cannot be identified internally or by

reaching in is it time to start trolling for candidates in advertise-ments in newspapers, professional journals, and other media.

Newspaper Advertising

Most people looking for jobs still check the newspaper first. Whether you run a local ad, run several regional ads, or adver-tise nationally in the *Wall Street Journal* depends on your willing-ness to pay for employee housing relocation.

Your ad's appearance is very important. You will be compet-ing against other ads for the reader's attention. Techniques such as borders and logos help, but white space is more important. Don't try to save 10 or 15 percent of the ad's costs by jamming everything into the smallest possible space. Leaving white space around the title and at other breaks in the text of your ad makes it easier to read and thus more likely to be read.

Always include your company's name in the ad. Blind ads put readers off, because people fear they may be sending their résumé to their own employer. A company that runs a blind ad to hide its recruiting from its employees is seriously underesti-mating its employees and is probably publishing an ad that is not specific enough to attract candidates who are solid matches. Don't succumb to the temptation. If you're worried that naming your company will encourage phone calls instead of résumés, clearly state that phone calls are not acceptable.

Developing the ad copy itself is straightforward if you fol-low this structure:

Title:	Start with the responsibility level, fol-lowed by the function.
	Manager, Accounts Receivable
Opening:	List the company name, type of busi-ness, location, job with duties or respon-sibilities.
	XYZ Company, a leading manufacturer of quality yo-yos, located in Chicago, needs an Accounts Receivable Manager to manage six-person dept.
Qualifications:	List all must-have job elements.

	Requires 5+ years experience in similar type or size co.
Payouts:	List salary and benefit information, and whether you will relocate candidates. *Competitive salary, benefits, and relocation packages.*
Contact:	List what information you want and where to send it. Ask for salary expectations instead of salary history to find what it will take to get the candidate. *Submit résumé, with salary expectations, to . . .*

Whether or not you should mention the starting salary depends on how firm you plan to be on that issue. If you absolutely will not pay outside a specific range, the range should be included. However, if you're not sure of the going rate for the position and you have some flexibility in the compensation area, don't mention exact figures. You will get more résumés in response to an ad without specific salary figures, so you'll have a greater field of candidates to review.

Most newspapers routinely place your ad on their Web page or on the Internet, which greatly increases your exposure.

Search/Employment Firms and Services

Use a search or employment firm when your organization:

- Doesn't have the time or the human resources to develop and place ads or to review résumés as they come in
- Doesn't want to or can't spend time prescreening applicants for qualifications and compensation level
- Wants to find candidates who are currently working for specific companies while remaining anonymous
- Wants access to a résumé file or database that may already include viable candidates

Search or employment firms and services operate on either a retainer or a contingency fee structure basis. A retainer structure means that the firm gets a percentage of the anticipated placement fee at the time it receives the search assignment. A retainer arrangement benefits the search firm because it is compensated for its research and prescreening work even if the client hires someone from another source. A retainer benefits the client because it ensures that the search firm dedicates itself to providing good candidates. The firm collects the balance of the placement fee only after an acceptable candidate is hired. This is the kind of "headhunter" to hire when you want to conduct a reach-in campaign or identify candidates for a high-level job.

An employment firm paid on a contingency basis is paid a fee only if you eventually hire one of the candidates it presents to you. Because the firm doesn't get the money up front, it is less committed to making your search successful—especially since many companies use several contingency search firms simultaneously *and* continue to advertise on their own.

Internet Advertising and Résumé Search Services

The Internet offers unlimited presentation and access opportunities to companies with open jobs and people who want to peruse job postings or post their own résumés. Linked with e-mail capabilities, this may be the ultimate job search environment, especially for large companies that can afford to post openings on their own Web pages and people who are comfortable cruising the Web.

Smaller companies may find it difficult to select from the wide variety of Internet employment services. Also, newspaper readers still outnumber computer owners, especially among blue-collar and trade workers, first-level supervisors, and salespeople. Until accessing the Internet becomes less dependent on owning your own computer, or until more people do own them, this technique will have limitations.

Trade and Professional Associations and Publications

Associations whose members are in the same field as your openings offer many opportunities to contact their membership. One reason that these associations exist is to help members get their names out in the market so that they can benefit from opportunities. They can provide membership lists or directories, lists of convention or seminar participants, as well as mailing labels—sorted by title, zip code, type of industry, or product line—that you can use to contact members at home.

Association newsletters or monthly bulletins are an excellent place to advertise for candidates. In addition, trade and professional magazines and newspapers often have job market sections where employment opportunities can be advertised. The costs are roughly the same as advertising in a newspaper. But this kind of publication offers two big advantages: Its readership is made up of exactly the kind of candidates you're looking for, and the ads are around for a longer period of time. If you are not familiar with the magazines and newspapers in your industry, ask a reference librarian for help in locating compatible publications.

Alumni Associations and School Bulletin Boards

Alumni associations and school bulletin boards exist to help students and graduates find jobs. Contact the schools that represent the occupation or professional base you're interested in and follow their procedures for posting your openings.

Radio and Cable Television Advertising

Radio advertising works best for situations requiring mass hiring in a local area. If you require production personnel; tradespeople; first-level supervisors; or office, clerical, warehouse, shipping, or delivery staff, it may be one of the most cost-effective advertising methods. Even if your target audience does not hear the broadcast, word will spread, and the papers or evening television news may pick it up as a local-interest filler item.

Cable television's ability to localize elements of broadcasting provides another opportunity for communicating with candidates. Low-cost commercials and/or "runners" at the bottom of the screen can give great visibility to multiple or mass employment openings. While any channel can run this type of advertising, most employment ads appear on information, preview, sports, or weather channels.

Networking

Another term for *networking* is *word-of-mouth advertising*. A few phone calls to business associates or a bulletin board announcement asking employees to help recruit for specific openings can get the word on the street very quickly. While networking is a very inexpensive way to identify candidates, you need to have a high tolerance for turning down friends of friends or relatives of employees.

Outplacement Firms

Firms hired by companies to assist terminated employees can be contacted for a list of the people they are helping to find gainful employment. Although these firms generally leave it up to the terminated person to contact companies, they are open to contact by you. Because the outplacement firm is paid by the company that hired it to provide transition assistance, there is never a fee for this service.

Temporary Employment Agencies

At one time, temporary employment agencies provided only people for the lower rungs of the employment hierarchy. Today there are few, if any, positions that cannot be filled with contract, temporary, or (as they are sometimes called) consultant help. Temporary employees may well be candidates for permanent positions within your organization. If they've been in your temporary employ for a while, their skills and work habits are already known to you, whereas the skills and work habits of outside candidates can be assessed only through somewhat tenuous reference checks. Check with your temporary agency to find out the kind of fee you need to pay to offer a permanent position to a temporary worker.

How Many Candidates Are Enough?

The initial search effort is the key to generating enough of a response to provide you with a sizable candidate base. The greater your effort and the larger the pool of applicants, the better the odds of finding viable candidates and making a successful choice.

What happens if the ideal candidate turns up early in the search? Some managers have no problem making an offer to the first credible person. Others want to see several candidates before they make an offer. Both of these practices are solid. The only bad practice is letting a candidate slip away because the process is dragged out to comply with a company search or hiring policy.

Don't prolong this search stage just to accumulate an arbitrary number of candidates or résumés. Move the good people through the interview process as soon as they surface. Your goal is to find the best candidate in the shortest time at the least expense.

CHAPTER 3

Filling the Job

People choose their occupations for three reasons. Some end up in an occupation by chance. When they start to look for work, they have nothing specific in mind. They simply take whatever job is available and, over the years, develop it into their career or trade or, with some resignation, just what they do for a living. A large percentage of the workforce operates this way. These people evaluate opportunities as they are presented and just expect things to develop through the years. Their jobs may not be a high-priority issue to them. They truly work to live, rather than live to work.

A second group enters a profession, trade, or business because they are exposed to it at an early age. Perhaps family members are in that field, or they learned about it in school and are guided in that direction. Many lawyers, engineers, plumbers, and police officers follow their parents' footsteps. Others simply join the family business.

The third group is made up of people with a strong interest, even passion, in a specific field or occupation. People don't become astronomers because it was the only job available or because it is the family business. They pursue it because astronomy brings excitement to their life and they can't imagine working in any other field.

Once qualifications and compensation have been determined, attitude is the final criterion for selecting a new hire. Appearance is also important, but I think appearance is a direct result of attitude. Appearance represents your attitude toward yourself, and attitude is important in every job. How people feel about their occupation directly affects how well they perform.

In the end, you want to hire someone whose attitude is geared toward performing tasks and accomplishing goals and objectives—the driving force in each and every employee in a successful organization.

While evaluating attitude is a very subjective exercise, determining qualifications is (or should be) objective. I find that hiring managers often have difficulties because they are either too subjective or too objective. The ideal selection technique utilizes both the subjective and the objective, but in the correct proportions and at the correct stages.

This chapter reviews the five steps in the candidate-selection process:

1. Using résumés to screen candidates
2. Interviewing candidates by telephone
3. Interviewing candidates face-to-face
4. Checking references
5. Making an offer

Using Résumés to Screen Candidates

The first step in candidate selection, reviewing résumés and determining whether candidates match targeted job requirements, should be purely objective. Either the résumé fits or it doesn't.

Résumés and cover letters are not easy to read, and you'll have too many to read each one cover to cover. On your first pass, you will need to develop a system for shifting the "yes" from the "no" résumés. The first thing to look for, of course, is the important *must-have* elements. The format and appearance of a résumé can also lead to the initial yes/no determination.

If a résumé is well formatted and has an interesting cover letter, but the candidate does not have the required qualifications, it should go into the reject pile. If the candidate meets the qualifications, but the résumé is poorly formatted and doesn't have a cover letter, it also goes into the reject pile. People who can't take the time to write a cover letter or present their résumé in a manner appropriate to the job level are not really interested in getting the job. Their résumés say, "I'm not much, but this makes me feel that at least I'm looking for work." Their attitude is *already* a problem. Don't devote any more time to these applicants.

Watch out for well-written résumés that represent marginally unacceptable individuals. Some résumés read like a ten-second television commercial. They sound good, but they're vague and they make it hard to determine the person's true qualifications. When you find one of these, pick up the phone. There is nothing wrong with calling and saying that you're in the initial stages of the candidate-selection process and just want answers to a couple of questions that came up during your first read of their résumé. Take the information and tell the candidate you'll be calling them later for a more in-depth discussion.

Yes and no résumés are easy to identify. It's the maybes that cause frustration. If your pile of yes résumés is large, you can afford to move quickly through the questionable ones. But when yes résumés are scarce, you can't afford to pass up any possibilities, so it is harder to discard résumés with potential value. Your only choice is to spend enough time on each résumé to determine whether it is good or questionable. There's no reason to go back for another review.

If your pile of yes résumés is discouragingly small, should you wait for résumés to come in? In general, the earlier the résumé, the better the candidate. But if you published your ad in the *Wall Street Journal*, you might wait for it to publish its weekly employment newspaper. Some excellent candidates buy this summary instead of daily issues of the newspaper. If you've advertised only in a local newspaper, there's no point waiting any longer. You'll have to try another method of identifying and attracting candidates.

Interviewing Candidates by Telephone

When you have divided your stack of résumés into a yes pile, a maybe pile, and a no pile, you are ready to begin the second step of the screening/selection process: conducting structured telephone interviews with the yes group. The purpose of these interviews is to screen candidates and decide, on the basis of the

Exhibit 3-1. Typical telephone interview guide.

Telephone Interview Guide

[*Author's note:* Although this form is designed to guide the telephone interviewer of applicants for the position of production supervisor at a laser manufacturing company, it is readily adaptable for use with candidates for various positions in various businesses.]

Job title _____

Name _____ Date _____

Compensation _____ Relocation _____

Experience

☐ Laser manufacturing _____

☐ Laser design _____

☐ Supervision _____

☐ Quality _____

Career objectives _____

Reason for leaving current/last job _____

_____

Current status _____

Communication skills _____

Claimed strengths _____

Admitted weaknesses _____

General comments _____

_____

Outcome of interview _____

interview outcome, if a candidate qualifies to go on to the next step of the process, the on-site, or face-to-face, interview. The telephone interview also provides an opportunity to "flesh out" any omissions and clarify any ambiguities in the person's résumé. Some key points to remember:

1. Ask the same questions and seek the same information in each telephone interview.
2. Avoid allowing the conversation to ramble, which can happen very easily, especially if you discover that the candidate and you share an interest or know the same people.
3. Remember to discuss all the key issues.

There is a surefire way to get consistent results from all your telephone interviews as well as to avoid both talking too much about nonpertinent matters and forgetting to get all the vital information you need: Develop and use a telephone interview guide, which is a form like the one shown in Exhibit 3-1. Following the guide's format will help you stay on track and ensure that you get must-have information, especially anything that will help you to determine whether to schedule an on-site interview.

Interviewing Candidates Face-to-Face

As with telephone interviews, your on-site interviews should be structured so as to get consistent information from the various candidates. Much of the basic information you are looking for is the same in both cases. However, you conduct the face-to-face interview with a smaller, more select group of candidates, one of whom will possibly be the person you hire. So where you can base your telephone interviews on a routine form like Exhibit 3-1, you need to do more extensive planning for your face-to-face interviews.

There are three key issues to account for in your plan so that you can address them during the interview:

Evaluating Work-Related Attitude and Drive

Getting people to reveal things about themselves during an interview that they don't realize are valuable to your decision is a real art. If you can initiate and conduct a conversation about the other person's outside interests or hobbies, you can gain considerable insight into that person. People with many hobbies or interests are telling you that they can learn and are interested in new experiences. People with leadership roles in many organizations are telling you that they see themselves as players. People with no outside activities are either observers or too busy or too lazy. Knowing how to gain this type of information is truly an advantage when it comes to determining the very best candidate from a stable of qualified people.

While knowledge is in the head, the real drive to do a job or pursue an outside activity comes from the heart. To hire the person with the best attitude and the greatest desire, you need to develop questions that evaluate these things. This isn't as intuitive as it sounds. To get the information you need to evaluate these qualities, learn to ask "Why?" five times on every issue that you want more insight into. Don't accept the first response to your question; ask "Why?" again. By the fourth or fifth "Why?" you will be at the heart of the issue—and the attitude, reason, or desire will be revealed.

You don't want to be overly aggressive, but you also should not worry about being obvious. You need to know. Individuals have standard, stylized responses to most questions asking why they do or did something, or why something happened to them. You need to get past these answers and into the specific, personalized justifications, rationalizations, and motivations to really learn about someone's attitude and desire.

This kind of probing interview style can sometimes result in polite disagreements. Don't let that bother you. Make it clear to the candidate that disagreements are not necessarily to be avoided. Two people who differ on or argue about an issue may often be closer on that issue than two people who do not disagree. Individuals who argue at least care about the issue, whereas those who don't argue may not even agree on its importance.

1. What the person has really done in previous jobs
2. How well that experience qualifies her or him to do what you want done in this job
3. What kind of attitude and how much energy this person will bring to this job (see the sidebar "Evaluating Work-Related Attitude and Drive," on page 33)

If you conduct an effective interview, you'll gather enough information about these three issues to determine whether you should consider making an offer to the interviewee. If you're not sure at the end of the meeting, either you have conducted a poor interview or you haven't found any reason to hire the person.

When you conduct a good interview, you know it. The results are there; either you feel like making an offer or you don't. Likewise, it's apparent when an interview goes poorly. There are seven major mistakes an interviewer can make, any one of which can run an interview off course. The first occurs during the planning process, the remaining six during the actual interview:

1. Failing to plan your interviews, that is, to structure them with clear objectives and a cogent outline.
2. Failing to follow the outline during the interview
3. Failing to get past the "stranger" stage with the candidate
4. Using interview time ineffectively and inefficiently
5. Talking too much—that is, listening too little
6. Relying too much on intuition or beliefs
7. Creating a stressful situation that drives away the candidate

Fortunately, these problems are easy to avoid.

Structure Your Interviews With Objectives and an Outline

The key to effective, face-to-face interviewing is to go into each interview with a well-structured plan. First develop clear objectives with respect to the critical issues you need to know more about, and write a basic outline designed to meet those objectives for each candidate you interview. Specifically, design the outline so that it deals with the *must-have* aspects of the job. These are the elements you will want to spend the most time on and get the most information about. Refer back to those items you identified when you defined the job and the ideal candidate. These issues should be transposed into open-ended interview questions that demand more than a simple yes or no response from every candidate you see.

The rest of the outline should be tailored to the individual candidate, containing questions based on the candidate's résumé that probe his or her experience and background. During the actual interview, the answers will confirm information given in the résumé and serve as a springboard for further questions. As the interview progresses and you learn important information about previous jobs, ask for and note those pertinent names of the interviewee's colleagues that do not appear on the résumé: supervisors, peers, and subordinates. Those people will make the most reliable references if and when you get to that stage.

To make sure you stick to your outline, rehearse the interview using it. Visualize how you'd like the interview to go by practicing your questions. Anticipate the various responses you might receive and how you will react to them. This exercise will help the interview go more smoothly, and will give you a benchmark by which you can measure the progress of the interview.

Stick to Your Outline

As you interview, follow your outline. Be sure to take notes during the discussion. Many interviewers want to adopt a casual demeanor and treat the session as if it were simply an unstructured conversation. It isn't. You need notes in order to accurately recall the particulars of each interview and person interviewed. Notes also tell you which items on your outline of objectives have been covered and how far you are in the interview. Without notes you may overlook important items on the list. Remember, the candidate, who also has an agenda for the interview, can cause you to shift your focus at times, and good notes will bring you back to where you left off.

If you deviate from the interview structure, you may not get the information you need to judge a candidate. Or you may find yourself indulging in small talk that creates an affinity for a candidate who, if the criteria in your objectives were applied, would not measure up.

Get Past the "Stranger" Stage

No one expects an employment interview to be the equivalent of a get-together between two long-lost friends, but there should be some feeling of common interest between you and the candidate. You already know the candidate's present and past employers, responsibilities, salary, schools, and hobbies. During the interview, you discover whether the person is happy on the job or, if he or she is unemployed, the reasons why. The candidate knows where you work, what you do, and, if the open job reports to you, roughly how much you earn. You are *not* two ships passing in the night. You already know more about each other than you would if you had met at a cocktail party. There should be some level of comfort between the two of you, considering all you know about one another.

But you don't need to worry if the chemistry just doesn't seem to be there. Stick to your interview outline. Focus on the issues you need to discuss. Keep digging. If you concentrate on the objective part of the qualification process, you will end up with a better feel for what the other person is like.

Use Your Time Wisely

Interviewers run out of time only when an interview isn't conducted in a structured manner. If you follow your outline, you will get the information you need to determine whether to accept or reject the person within the allotted time. But don't embarrass an obvious reject by sending him or her on the way after a short talk. Use the extra time to go back over key items in an effort to make sure of your impressions.

Talk Less and Listen More!

The more talking you do, the less information you will receive. Your role is that of a buyer. You are thinking about purchasing

---

Assessing Communication Skills: The 3-by-5 Card Test

Because an interview is an exercise in communication, the interview is the perfect time to determine whether the candidate meets the communication requirements for the job. To find the candidate's communication strengths, ask yourself whether the candidate could:

- ❏ *Reduce* a 100-page report to a single 3-by-5 card.
- ❏ *Expand* the information on a 3-by-5 card into a 100-page report.

Depending on the nature of the job to be filled, one or both of these skills may be advantageous. The ability to be brief and to the point can be an advantage in some situations; to be terse about everything and in every situation can be detrimental. The tendency to embellish a response when a simple yes or no will do may annoy you, unless you're hiring a trade show representative. To be able to continue talking about your product when the question was simply "How long have you been producing these?" can be a real asset.

---

services from the person you're interviewing. Asking questions and evaluating the responses are your key functions. Picture yourself at a car dealership, talking to a salesperson about the possible purchase of a car. Who should be doing most of the talking? Who should be answering the most questions? In both cases the answer is the person selling, not the person buying. The person asking the questions gets the most information. In the initial employment interview, you should do only about 25 percent of the talking, and most of your talking should be questions. In a subsequent interview, where you are offering the job and trying to get the person to join your company, the roles may be reversed.

Your questions should seek information on specific issues and also let you uncover personality traits. Listen for comments that indicate attitudes, energy levels, and the ability to communicate concisely and to answer the question asked, not the one the interviewee wants to answer (see the sidebar "Assessing Communication Skills: The 3-by-5 Card Test," on page 37). None of this can be accomplished when you are doing the majority of the talking.

Don't Overrely on Intuition

Research indicates that as much as 80 percent of all communication between people is nonverbal. During the first three or four minutes of an interview, almost all of your impressions are based on a candidate's nonverbal presentation. From that point on, you begin to focus on content, but your first impressions act as a screen through which all subsequent data are processed.

If you think the other person has a hairpiece or wig, this impression will influence the way you interpret other information. If he or she is trying to fool people with that hairpiece, what else might be being covered up? An interviewer may see a nervous candidate as hiding something or as unable to deal with the stress of the interview. A candidate whose style is laid back and casual may be thought insincere about getting the job or too experienced at interviewing. The candidate's body language can also contribute negatively—or positively—to the interviewer's first impressions.

Even though these issues shouldn't be given the weight that

Preemployment Testing

Inexperienced people are difficult to evaluate and experienced people are difficult to retrain, but everyone can be tested. Consider hiring a testing service to develop and conduct appropriate tests for all serious candidates. Organizations such as Wonderlic and Stanford-Binet have industry-specific tests as well as generalized intelligence tests with universal application. These tests can pinpoint and reveal aspects that most of us can only guess at. They are well worth the expense, no matter how heavy or light your hiring activity.

experience and skills are given, our intuition begs to be utilized. We can't use it to influence objective information, so we apply it elsewhere, whether it is needed or not. The cracks between the facts are filled with intuition, and sometimes this can work against us by distorting our objective judgment. Unfortunately, a significant portion of the decisions resulting from employment interviews are based on what interviewers think they saw or heard and how that fits with what they would like to have seen or heard.

If you rely on intuition and hunches, you may overlook a highly qualified candidate. Instead of focusing on personality issues and first impressions, focus on your outline and your objectives. Personality, body language, and nonverbal signs may be interesting, but they aren't what you are after at this point in the interview process. Ask the questions you have developed and listen to the answers you get. Take notes and evaluate the person against your criteria. If you do, you won't inadvertently dismiss a good candidate because of your first impressions.

A reliable way to avoid basing interview and hiring decisions on your intuitive insights—whether negative or positive—is to have all serious candidates undergo preemployment testing (see the sidebar "Preemployment Testing," on page 38).

Avoid the Stress Interview and the "Group Grope"

If a position to be filled requires the jobholder to deal with considerable stress, some interviewers attempt to create a stressful environment during the initial interview. They may ask rapid-fire questions that are severely direct, challenge the candidate's responses, or have two or three other people take turns asking questions. Although their intent is to discover the candidate's ability to cope with stress, they almost always fail to do so. While something may be revealed, it seldom has anything to do with the ability to handle on-the-job situations. The objective of the interview shifts from trying to gather real information to trying to create an emotional reaction.

The ability to handle stressful situations is a function of experience, knowledge, and preparation. The best way to probe the ability to handle stress is to discuss the candidate's typical exposure to tight schedules or demanding customer expectations. Trying to create stress during the interview will only make the candidate think you're trying to run him or her out the door.

Another technique to avoid is the "group grope," in which people other than the hiring manager are brought into the interview process to pass judgment on the candidates or even recommend a finalist. I don't see any reason why hiring managers would want to use this technique unless company policy dictates it. In my opinion, asking peers to be part of your hiring process is like asking someone else to pack your parachute. Why ask other people to do your job, especially if they don't have your level of knowledge or passion for quality?

It's one thing if your superior wants to be part of the decision. He or she probably has the judgment and the motivation to protect your best interests. But extending the interviewing to your peers, the candidate's potential peers, or an upper-management team just doesn't make sense. Get too many people involved in the process and you'll end up with a candidate designed by a committee—a candidate who may mean all things to all people, except the one thing you're looking for. Managers seek to create competition within their department or between departments because competition adds to performance. Committees, on the other hand, tend to want to prevent or weed out competition.

If others don't know as much as you do about what is needed in the job, and their interests aren't the same as yours, why waste everyone's time by involving them? As the hiring manager, why let the candidate believe you're indecisive or not in control? You don't delegate responsibility for the employee once he or she is on board. Don't delegate responsibility for hiring him or her.

Checking References

Checking references is frustrating. It's hard to get through to people, and when you reach them, their comments may be cursory. Still, it's important to check references on every serious candidate. Avoid personal references; use only job-related references, preferably those that were noted during the interview discussions. Don't delegate reference checking to someone else simply because you expect to get only employment dates and job titles. Make the calls yourself. Try to get through to the previous supervisors and to get some information, no matter how limited. If company policy allows it and the employee was a good performer, you will get what you need.

Because it's difficult to talk to the supervisors of final candidates who are currently employed, some managers give their references only a cursory check, or skip them altogether. Their reluctance stems from fear of losing the candidate. They'd rather get the person on board and hope for the best.

I think that's foolhardy. References of a final candidate should *always* be checked. When your number-one candidate is employed elsewhere, follow this procedure:

1. Tell the candidate that your job offer is contingent upon good references that confirm what he or she has said in the interview.
2. Make it clear that if your offer is accepted, the candidate is expected to resign from his or her current job.
3. Your company will then follow up with a reference check regarding dates of employment, responsibilities, and salary level.

Describing this procedure up front lets the candidate know that you value honesty and integrity and that falsification of any kind will cancel the job offer.

Consider a personal visit for a reference check if the position is critical enough. You might also want to use a reference check service and have the candidate sign a release permitting the checks.

Never compromise your standards if you hear something that you don't like during the reference check. Remember, performance history is the best indicator of future performance.

Making the Offer

Consider the plight of a young lion hunting an antelope for dinner. The lion gazes through the tall grass at a herd of over a thousand antelopes, thinking that he'll never go hungry again with all these antelopes around. The lion charges one of the most "qualified" antelopes and chases it for a while. When he realizes that this antelope may not be catchable, he stops running and looks around for another candidate, only to find that the other antelopes have all gone somewhere else.

The first antelope now has too great an advantage, and to continue chasing it would be too costly. And while the supply of antelopes is more than adequate, their availability to the lion depends on the lion's speed in securing the first candidate he goes after. The lion must quickly turn away from any antelope he's not sure he can catch before the other antelopes have all disappeared.

Too many managers operate as if the candidate base, like the supply of antelopes, is static. It isn't. The candidates you like and put on hold while you interview others may no longer be there when you try to go back to them. The odds of finding and hiring the absolute best candidate out there are very slim. That person is probably also interviewing somewhere else. The odds of getting the best candidate from your pool are better, depending on the size of your candidate pool. If you insist on having six to eight exceptional candidates, you'll spend so much time on interviews that the first one may get away by the time you get around to making an offer.

If you want to see a number of good people, you will have to compress the process into a shorter time period or make an offer to someone you feel is *a* winner, even if not necessarily *the* winner, as soon as you realize this. Remember, your objective is not to conduct interviews but to fill the job with a person who meets your qualifications. If you did a good job identifying those qualifications, you'll be ready to make an offer to someone who meets them, no matter how early in the search that person turns up. Doing the groundwork up front saves you valuable time at this stage of the hiring process.

If your very first candidate is ideal, should you make an offer or wait? The answer depends on whether you have other candidates who are just as good. If you don't, don't spend time looking for them; make the offer. After all, just because you make an offer of employment doesn't mean that the person will accept. See and evaluate other candidates in the interview pipeline within three days or less. In other words, you should make an offer within three days of seeing a solid candidate. Better yet, make it right away if you are really comfortable with the match.

What happens if the candidate does not feel that the offer is good enough? Make one more try, but have the candidate give you an example of what he or she feels is a fair offer. You don't want to be negotiating against yourself. You may have to sweeten the offer to something that you feel is fair. If the answer is still negative, quickly go to the next candidate.

The Offer Letter

When you write a letter to the potential new hire making the job offer and providing acceptance criteria, keep these points in mind:

❑ Be careful not to commit the company to a binding employment agreement that is both misleading and unintentional. Avoid any implied contract of employment by expressing salary dollars in weekly or monthly amounts, rather than annual figures. This may prevent the employee's claiming a full year's salary should termination occur before year-end. Including a statement that employment can be severed by either party for any reason, at will, may not be necessary if your company has an employee handbook or policy manual stating this.

❑ Before you commit your salary offer to paper, consider its impact on the earnings of current employees in jobs that are similar or the same. If the new hire's starting pay is similar to salaries for senior people in the same area, you may create internal salary problems.

❑ Include an offer pullback date. You need to know within a day or two if the offer is going to be rejected so that you can move on to the other candidates before they slip away.

❑ Include a line for the candidate to initial or sign to indicate that the offer was accepted as outlined in the letter.

What If They're Not Out There?

If you attract candidates but can't get them interested in your company or your offer, you may have one or several problems. Asking for feedback from the lost candidates should give you some insight into whether the problem is workplace location or conditions, type of company product or service, salary range, benefits, or your interview style. But if you haven't had a reasonable response to the recruiting effort, the problem is probably in one of two areas: Either the opening is poorly described in the ad copy, or the job itself is not common to the labor market.

It's easy to rewrite poor ad copy. But if the job isn't common, you may need to rethink the job. Before you do, check a compensation survey that discloses salaries in common "benchmark" jobs. If the position is listed, it should have enough representation in the job market to enable you to generate candidates. If it's not, you may need to redesign the responsibilities or try to fill the position from inside.

The heart and soul of the selection process is accurate definition of the job to be filled. Without an accurate definition, a manager cannot hope to find viable, matching candidates. And unless candidates can be accurately matched to a job they are qualified to perform satisfactorily, there is little assurance that they will perform as you would like them to once they are hired. The result is often marginally performing employees or turnover—both of which are costly to the organization and harmful to the hiring manager's performance and career.

PART TWO

Direct

The main reason managers don't get the results they want from the people they supervise is that they haven't clearly defined those results ahead of time.

Suppose you tell your ten-year-old to clean up his room and get everything off the floor. When you check the room, this goal appears to have been achieved—until you open the closet and trigger an avalanche of toys and clothes. Who's to blame? You are. You failed to mention that the closet is considered part of the bedroom. You assumed that your child understood the broader picture, when he was simply doing what you said to do and little more. You failed to give adequate direction.

Direction is the effective management of the performance of people and equipment in the accomplishment of the organization's overall objectives.

Organizations hire people to assist in reaching company goals and objectives. Managers are hired to direct employee efforts in accomplishing those objectives. Saying "Do your best" is not sufficient if you're a manager. There are too many ways to interpret a vague statement like this, and you can bet that the end result won't be what you want.

The best kind of direction is derived from a strategic plan that clearly outlines a company's goals and objectives. This section tells how to develop a strategic plan–based direction program that embraces everyone at every level of your company. It explains why direction is necessary, how to derive direction from a business plan, and how to train managers and employees alike in making sure that everyday, on-the-job activities achieve results that move the company toward its goals.

CHAPTER 4

Determining Direction

Direction begins with a strategic or business plan that outlines the principal products and services a business wants to produce for a specified market over a specified period of time.

A strategic plan and its objectives define a business. A company may build cars, but it can't define its business until it can pinpoint whether it intends to build economically priced, entry-level cars for first-time buyers and compete on a worldwide basis through distribution and service, or it intends to build a handful of very expensive, highly customized cars for a select group of wealthy customers.

Until a business can define its objectives, employees won't know whether building one car or 5,000 is acceptable. Until it can pinpoint its market, an employee told to set up a distribution system won't know whether to set one up for a city, a state, a region, or the globe.

The strategic plan defines the business, and its objectives will determine the direction you as a manager and your company need to take. Without a strategic plan, a business will have little or no formal notion of where it is going and will not be able to communicate its goals and objectives throughout the organization. But with a strategic plan, a company can translate these overall goals and objectives into accomplishable actions.

These company objectives influence every step in selecting, directing, evaluating, and rewarding: selecting, because objectives help you design jobs and find the people who can do those jobs best; directing, because those objectives tell employees how to spend their time on the job; evaluating, because measuring goals and objectives is the basis for evaluating a person's performance; and rewarding, because salaries should be tied to goals. Tell people on the plant floor that you are going to install a new pay program, and they may wonder about your motives. Tell them that the company is trying to increase profits from 3 to 6 percent and that the pay program will reward actions that save money through more effective procedures, and they'll understand.

While all businesses have strategic objectives, a formal strategic plan concisely commits to paper goals and objectives that are understandable, measurable, and achievable. Typical areas in which objectives are set include:

- Increasing profits
- Reducing costs
- Introducing new products
- Outsourcing specific functions
- Expanding operations
- Acquiring similar businesses
- Penetrating offshore markets
- Upgrading equipment
- Reducing turnover
- Automating operations

It is management's responsibility to break down these broad objectives into smaller elements and assignments and translate them into jobs within the organization. The more effectively these elements and assignments are identified and communicated, the greater the chance that the objectives will be achieved.

You can't simply tell people that the company has to make more profit or reduce costs. Instead, you need to break down the objective or objectives into understandable and practical tasks and assignments. In my opinion, *every* job needs to be connected to the business plan. As a manager, you have the job of showing employees the connection between their jobs and company goals so that those objectives can be accomplished.

In my view, the strategic plan is brought to life by translating objectives into specific responsibilities in the following manner:

1. The company creates an overall business plan, with specific objectives and deadlines.
2. The business plan is communicated to all management levels.
3. The business plan is translated into functional or departmental objectives.
4. Managers identify specific jobs that are required to meet those objectives, and set objectives for individuals or job classifications.
5. Managers create milestones marking progress toward objectives.
6. Managers monitor progress in jobs.
7. Managers identify and initiate appropriate action steps required to maintain focus.

This, in a nutshell, is direction. When it takes place effectively at every level of the organization, it creates the energy that is essential to the success of the organization and its parts. It does so by creating pressure in areas that are essential to meeting the objectives in the business plan.

As this list of tasks makes clear, direction depends on managers. Thus, if your company's goal is to increase profit, it's your job to focus your employees on tasks that lower costs and increase revenue. It's also your job to tell them *why* these tasks are important and how they relate to your company's overall objectives. If your employees don't know what to do and why, they may concentrate on other tasks altogether. Activity that isn't directed at the proper goals and objectives wastes time and effort.

Why Direction Is Important

Neither automated equipment, advanced systems, nor manpower can replace good, detailed direction of employees. What Frederick Taylor, the man often identified as the father of scientific management, said in 1911 still holds true today: "A good organization with a poor plant will give better results than the best plant with a poor organization." No matter how impressive the technology or plant, the deck is stacked against a poorly directed company.

Imagine two military commanders giving instructions. One says, "March as hard as you can and we'll stop at nightfall to evaluate our progress." The other says, "March to the river, cross it, set up camp, and establish a defensive perimeter. At that point we'll eat and determine our next objective." The first commander is saying, in effect, that his troops will work and then look backward at what they've accomplished, hoping it will have been a good effort. The second commander won't have to look backward because everyone will know what was accomplished that day. He will be able to plan for the next day. That's what managers should do. You are paid to lead people to certain places, not simply to trail after them and determine their progress.

Clear direction benefits a company in many ways:

- It helps orient new employees to their tasks by letting them know what is required so that they don't waste time on activities that do not make progress toward a goal.
- It creates a "can do" attitude throughout the organization. When goals, targets, problems, or opportunities are clear, employees can focus their energies on solving them. Being directed toward a highly focused set of tasks is very motivating for people who like to work in a challenging situation.
- It creates an exciting culture in which results are measured, milestones are celebrated, and constant growth reinforces and rewards everyone's effort.
- It allows the company to quickly respond to changes or surprises in the environment.
- It makes it easier to evaluate performance. Detailed direction establishes clear performance standards and expectations for the company, the department, and the individual.
- It creates and attracts a better workforce. Setting, main-

taining, and communicating high but attainable standards for performance causes employees to become more productive. High standards also make employees feel more pride in the company and attract candidates who know that the organization is a notch or two above the average. Strong candidates are attracted to companies with high standards; weaker people may not even consider applying!

❑ It facilitates teamwork. Teamwork comes about almost automatically in a well-directed organization. All employees know the key objectives of the business, their function or department, and their individual job. They know and understand the part they play in those objectives and the responsibilities and roles of others. Because everyone is directed at the same prize, efforts are coordinated. Teamwork is built into the system.

❑ It reduces difficulties involving personality differences or workforce diversity. Strong direction keeps the emphasis on performance, not personality. When problems flare up during times of high stress or pressure, people will be more likely to push them aside and stay focused on the higher issues.

❑ It builds loyalty. Employees usually feel a stronger allegiance to their coworkers than to their bosses or the company as a whole. But directing them toward common business-unit goals and objectives unifies a workforce and creates a real sense of commitment.

❑ It helps managers manage consistently instead of in spurts. Too many managers are reactive. They engage in flurries of attention and activity whenever they see things slipping away, or important problems or projects not getting the necessary attention. Direction helps managers consistently identify, communicate, and direct attention to critical short- and long-term issues. Continual light pressure is less intense, more balanced, and more effective than brief periods of heavy or extreme pressure.

❑ It makes deadlines easier to meet. An executive of IBM was asked during a stockholders' meeting just how an important project could have been delayed a full year. His reply: "One day at a time." When direction is strong and consistent and managers make sure that tasks are focused on objectives, deadlines don't slip.

❑ It leads to frequent, visible accomplishments, or "little victories," that motivate employees and keep them focused on their goals. A lack of accomplishments is like fishing without catching any fish; eventually the fisherman dozes off in the sunshine, and others catch the fish.

Why Managers Don't Give Proper Direction

The movie *Patton* contains a scene in which General George Patton's army is stalled at a narrow bridge while attempting to move in the direction of the enemy. As he approaches in his command car, Patton realizes that there is a bottleneck and makes his way through the troops to find out why. The bridge is blocked by a cart and two mules who are resisting every effort of their driver and a number of soldiers to urge them forward.

General Patton doesn't waste any time assembling a team to look into the problem or empowering his staff to decide what should be done. Instead, he unholsters one of his ivory-handled sidearms and shoots each mule in the head. He then has the dead mules and the cart tossed over the side of the bridge so that his troops can advance toward their objective.

General Patton's job was to see the problem in the context of the overall mission objective, which did not include spending any significant time on the movement or survival of livestock. Likewise, management's primary responsibility is to view every task, job, problem, or opportunity in terms of its significance within the company's short- and long-range business plans.

Unfortunately, many managers spend too much time fighting fires and resolving operational issues and not enough time directing their employees in terms of the Grand Plan. They also confuse being busy and working hard with meeting the goals of the company. But activity alone is not enough. In many cases, activity may even camouflage a company's lack of progress toward its goals and objectives.

Whether they are first-level supervisors or vice presidents, managers have three basic responsibilities when it comes to managing their workforce. It's their job to:

1. Direct employees toward objectives.
2. Oversee the work effort and address immediate problems.
3. Report information on the progress of the work to their superiors.

Responsibility number two is relatively easy to accomplish. Overseeing day-to-day activity and addressing problems gives managers an opportunity to exhibit their expertise. They can operate in a very hands-on manner and reinforce their importance to the department, or they can stay in their office and, like a mayor, receive people who come to them for advice and guidance. Their ego is stroked with every visit.

Responsibility number three consumes little time today, thanks to computers that capture the number of units shipped, number of tons produced, number of service calls performed, and so on, and makes these data accessible to everyone in the loop. Manual tracking and report development (once an essential function of managers) is no longer necessary.

This brings us back to responsibility number one. Direction toward objectives can be a difficult and risky task. It's tough to translate performance objectives into challenging but reachable targets that are relevant to the overall business plan. In fact, setting performance and business plan–related goals can set managers up for failure if employees fail to reach the objectives. No wonder so many managers avoid stressing this part of their job.

When managers avoid this responsibility, it's either because they haven't been trained to and *can't* translate business objectives into department or individual objectives, or because they *won't* voluntarily risk setting themselves up for any degree of failure.

It takes a very self-confident and aggressive person to direct employees toward business-related goals and objectives with deadlines. Those who do have the best chance of reaching top management positions.

A Few Words About Goals and Process

Directing from the strategic plan is a goal-setting process. And goal setting means change. It means doing things differently so that more is achieved or less is expended, or doing new things altogether so that new markets and territories are explored. Direction is focused on results.

People, on the other hand, focus on process, because they hate change. To preserve order in their work environment, they try to eliminate potential surprises and avoid situations they may not be prepared to handle. Managers and nonmanagers alike focus on process, establishing systems or procedures that will do defined tasks as efficiently as they think possible. Too often these complex systems and procedures become the proverbial gatekeeper that dictates what can and cannot be done or accepted in that department or system. Information or services that cannot be provided by the present process are hard or impossible to get. The process determines whether the requested information or service is produced or provided, not the value or benefit that would be derived by fulfilling that request.

Process makes people feel comfortable, but because it focuses on maintaining previous objectives rather than accomplishing future objectives, it can stop the goal-setting process dead in its tracks. Thus, even though top management may be trying to move the organization forward, the middle and first levels of management may be doing all they can to preserve and protect the present! This low-risk, protective tendency has to be addressed and overcome before all managers will direct on the basis of the company's overall, and ever changing, business plans.

Processes aren't sacred, so don't protect them. It's your job to improve results, not to maintain the status quo. Let people know that the processes in place may not represent the best way to do things. Encourage them to question every step in their work process to see if it is still valid or if there is a way to do things better, faster, or more accurately. Your objective is to do whatever is necessary to reach the company's strategic or business plan, not to manage processes that are currently in place. By taking direction from goals and objectives, you can stay focused on the results and alter or adjust processes as necessary.

Can There Be Too Much Direction?

While exercise is beneficial to our health and quality of life, excessive amounts can cause injury or chronic fatigue. Likewise, realistic direction of employees toward the overall business plan will create a healthy company culture, but too much will cut into the organization's muscle and weaken or destroy it. What might have taken years to build or grow can be permanently damaged by expectations and pressure beyond the capabilities or the willingness of the workforce to endure.

The state of the business indicates whether more or less direction is necessary. If the company is growing at a rate that is comparable to, or better than, the competition's, the direction is probably adequate, although there's always room for improvement. But if company growth is below what it should be, and the competition is gaining, passing, or pulling further ahead, then more direction is necessary. When the battle is being lost and the future looks bleak, there's no such thing as too much pressure or superhuman goals and objectives. Fallout—personnel burnout or terminations and replacements by those who can perform at higher levels of intensity—may be excused because the jobs of many are at risk. When the situation is dire, casualties are to be expected.

Direction overload may occur when a company's objectives are realistic but the time designated for the accomplishment of those objectives is not. These companies seem to be continually in the "white-water rapids" of direction, always thrashing desperately to stay afloat. Instead of taking the time to plan ahead, they handle each mile of the river as it comes. As they constantly deal with unexpected problems or situations, their future is no further than the next rock or wave. The direction required in these situations is extreme in its intensity and has a very short time horizon. This is reaction, not direction.

Reserves of energy and knowledge need to be saved for emergency situations, not used up beforehand. Pushing people to continually perform at their maximum level is not wise human resource management. Workers who receive too much direction may become aggressive and independent in unproductive ways. They may back off from their efforts at noncritical moments or find other ways, such as attempts at unionization, to let management know that the pressure is too great.

The irony is that companies have to plan, set goals, and reach those goals in order to be considered successful. Humans, on the other hand, support philosophies that stress that becoming a millionaire or a saint is not important. Instead, what counts is how hard you work and how you live your life in terms of family and others. In other words, it's the journey that matters, not the measurable, objective results.

Business stresses results; people stress methods. The only way to deal with this fundamental contradiction is to identify it and justify it to employees through education and management awareness.

Determining What to Direct

Direction comes from reality. When you set objectives and translate them into action steps to be performed by employees, you need to make sure that what you are asking your employees to do addresses your company's reality.

All people operate within two different frames of reference: perception and reality. How they perceive reality and how well they identify reality and know it when they see it determines how they direct their lives in general.

Someone who is struggling with a poorly written textbook may think, "I'm just no good at math" instead of recognizing that the book is the problem. That person may arrange his or her life in a way that avoids or eliminates math. Because there are alternatives to using math when it comes to making a living, the person may operate successfully on the basis of the perception that he or she is dumb at math, not on the reality that the material was poorly presented.

Businesses don't have the luxury of avoiding reality in favor of perception. In business, reality must prevail. Management's first job is always to define the realities of the external market and the realities of the company's internal operations. A business can't survive long if management ignores the market or the business's organization in providing its product or service.

You need to accurately determine just what your company is up against in terms of the competition and the marketplace. You also need to evaluate your company's internal capabilities—equipment, staff, finances, etc.—and determine how effectively they can deal with that external reality. In a sense, it's your job to overlay the internal on the external and address those areas that do not match. Since it's hard to induce external factors to change, you'll have to seek ways to mold the internal factors to conform to them. Once you understand what is happening in a market, you can develop a business plan to deal with the reality.

A manager's primary job is to define reality inside and outside the company. A perception like "I think we're doing great in the marketplace" just won't fly. External reality and internal efforts simply must match. Too often, when things outside are changing, internal factors stay the same. Back in the 1980s IBM misread the PC market because, as the biggest dog on the block, it assumed that it was determining the marketplace. Too late, it discovered that consumer tastes were changing and that its internal procedures were set up for a market that no longer was real. Too many of its engineers, technicians, and sales and customer service people were addressing only a perceived reality. It took a major effort for IBM to redesign itself to address the actual reality.

Measurement is one way to define and determine reality, because it strips away perception to expose as much reality as is possible. When you don't feel that someone is trying hard enough, you are dealing in perception. When you tell that person that he or she didn't produce enough widgets today, you are dealing in a measured reality. The more you measure, the more you can manage. You can set practical goals and objectives only in areas where you have identified and measured reality.

Many managers find this aspect of management challenging and intimidating. They feel more comfortable dealing with the daily operational problems that employees or customers present to them, when what they need to do is extend themselves into the risky area of measuring reality, setting objectives based on that reality, measuring the progress or performance of the organization or individual, and setting new objectives. This process, repeated over and over, is management.

Daily operational problems will continue indefinitely when managers address them only as they surface. Sooner or later, however, it's necessary to begin to measure the effect those problems are having on the business and find ways to reduce or eliminate them. As Peter Drucker says, "The fundamental problem is the reality around the executive. Unless he changes it by deliberate action, the flow of events will determine what he is concerned with and what he does."

Directing people means identifying and focusing them on the total set of objectives, based on the business plan, that management requires or desires. Thus, when top management identifies profit improvement as a primary goal for the coming year, that goal is translated into lower-level initiatives that seek to reduce or eliminate daily operational problems by redesigning the systems within which they occur.

Direction works when everyone understands how her or his work relates to the real objective or focus of the business. It corrects problems that arise when objectives are not sufficiently communicated from level to level. For example, the credit manager for a small business may see her job as giving credit only to potential customers who meet strict criteria. As a result, she may turn away some of the business that salespeople bring in. The president, on the other hand, knows that there are start-up companies whose cash flow may not permit them to pay within a certain period but that always pay eventually. In the president's mind, these customers represent significant long-term opportunities and should not be turned away. There's a gap here—a 30 percent gap, according to management consultant George Odiorne, between what the boss thinks a job should do and what the employee thinks a job should do.

If this 30 percent gap exists from one level to the next, imagine the size of the gap between top management and the lowest levels in the organization. Unless direction is clear, focus is gradually eroded as instructions are issued from the top. This erosion also affects the evaluation process. A significant segment of the workforce—managers included—is always surprised to discover the job aspects that they are being evaluated against. They were not aware that their superiors were looking for certain new results or efforts in addition to the results they normally accomplish. These surprises come when higher-level objectives are not translated and disseminated throughout the organization. That's why it's important to make sure you make clear just what standards or measurements are being used to evaluate people and departments.

Management: A Top-Down Affair

A business plan is applied on four levels:

1. The company level
2. The function level
3. The departmental level
4. The individual employee level

Each of these levels requires its own translation or definition of the elements in the business plan. Here's how a single company objective might be translated and assigned down through the organization.

Company-Level Objective

Increase profits an additional 2 percent (total of 8 percent) of sales.

Function-Level Objectives

Sales & Marketing Function: Increase sales of high-profit products by 20 percent.

Manufacturing Function: Increase productivity by 10 percent.

Departmental-Level Objectives

Sales Department: Train sales staff in promotion/sales of high-profit products.
Assembly Department: Develop and install gain-sharing incentive pay program.

Individual-Level Objectives

Salesperson: Establish 20 percent higher targets for specific product sales per person.
Assemblers: Establish and train teams of assemblers in gain-sharing goals.

As management at each level sets its objectives, it needs to translate those objectives into actions relative to that level's responsibilities in the company, communicate to and direct the employees at that level in the accomplishment of the objectives, and then measure progress and take appropriate action to ensure performance.

Top management almost always focuses on internal growth issues: the issues or problems that need to be addressed within the company. Without direction, lower levels of management won't grasp those internal growth issues completely. They may feel that simply working harder at what they are currently doing will meet top management's requirements. The reality is that entirely new and additional efforts or goals will have to be developed and met if growth is to occur.

By no means are all of middle- and lower-level management's objectives determined at the top of the organization. All levels of management have the responsibility of setting their own objectives based on their own operating problems and challenges. However, all levels must make room for overall business growth goals and the extra burdens that these goals place on functions, departments, and individuals. The issues that determine the direction given employees have to encompass functional, departmental, and individual goals and objectives as well as overall company targets.

Still, management is a top-down affair. Goals and objectives set at the top need to be translated to these four levels so that they eventually encompass everyone in the company. In my view, too many businesses and managers try to work from the bottom up by focusing only on what is happening around them. They take over an ongoing situation, decide to work closely with subordinates to address their problems, and end up spending their time on issues that have little to do with the company's big-picture problems and opportunities.

To succeed, a manager needs to not merely maintain what is already happening or simply solve problems surrounding him or her, but make sure that all activities are tied to company objectives. It's top management's job to make sure that the company sets goals and then uses them as the basis for effective direction.

CHAPTER 5

Training Management in Direction

For many years, Portuguese dory fishermen plied their trade in a unique manner. A "mother ship" would depart from Portugal with as many as sixty one-man dories on board. Once the ship arrived at the fishing grounds, the one-man dories and their occupants were lowered overboard to spend the day fishing over a broad area with land lines strung with 400 to 1,000 hooks. Because a single dory could catch bigger fish and cover almost as much area in a day as the mother ship, sixty dories would, as a group, provide a greater catch.

The fishermen's objective was to fill the ship's hold with fish as fast as possible. That goal was translated into smaller action steps—dispatching sixty dories that accomplished the job quickly, but not without danger. Being alone on the ocean in a one-man boat is always hazardous. Often, the fishermen would be engulfed in fog and unable to find their way back to the mother ship. This made for some long and damp nights for those unfortunate anglers, many of whom never did find the ship the next morning.

But the fishermen were prepared for the hardships standing between them and their objective. In essence, these men had been trained. Raised in fishing families, they had been taught how to handle a boat, string a fish line, and understand the weather and the elements. They were qualified for the job before they ever sailed off alone in a dory, and they were further trained by older fishermen who showed them the day-to-day procedures of fishing in this manner.

Fortunately, sonar technology has made this practice of overloading the area with individual boats obsolete. But commercial fishermen are still out there to bring back fish, and they are trained as carefully as ever to meet the overall objective. Only the jobs, processes, and tools used to catch fish have changed.

Training is the first step in teaching people to bring back fish. It's the best form of direction a company can give, because it tells people what you want them to do and how you want them to do it. Training is not a luxury or an expense that can be put off for later. It is part and parcel of directing people.

Certainly training is required whenever new products are being introduced or new technology is purchased and installed. In order to profit from an investment, a company must teach its employees how to get the most from capital equipment. But I believe that every company should also take the time to train its people in the contents of its business plan every single year. To be effective, the program should translate companywide goals and objectives into specific tasks that enable employees to accomplish those objectives.

Two annual training programs are needed in order to achieve company objectives: one for managers and one for nonmanagers. Managers need to learn how to take directions from above and also how to direct those below them in day-to-day activities that are driven by a strategic plan. Nonmanagement employees need to be trained in how to perform the activities that will ultimately accomplish the company's strategic goals. This chapter focuses on the process of developing and installing a training program for managers at all levels of the company.

Why Training Is Necessary

Is it really necessary to formally train managers in how to direct? If directions are clear and thorough, won't you get the results you want? Maybe. But directions often are not clear and not thorough. And simply giving clear and thorough directions is not enough. You also have to consider the number of assignments and the amount of time allowed for each if you are to have any idea as to the eventual effectiveness of the directions given. A still deeper issue is the purpose of the directions.

The purpose of any training program is to translate knowledge into action—to provide new information and show how to use that information on the job. It also creates expertise—in this case, the expertise that permits the accomplishments that move a business toward its objectives. The purpose of expertise is to get things done quickly. If we know how to do something without trial and error, and we do it correctly the first time, we get that thing done sooner, without having to develop techniques as we go along. Training in "direction expertise" allows us to quickly determine and channel the activities of the organization toward its goals.

The winner in a race isn't always the fastest person; it is often the person who knows the most direct route and who slows down the fewest times. This should be the goal of direction training: to show the most direct route and to provide the expertise so that management and nonmanagement personnel can operate without slowing down in order to determine, or reestablish, direction and focus.

We equip employees in the business world through training and experience. Experience can be costly. In fact, it can be a difficult enemy. People carry a considerable amount of baggage as they move through their careers. This experience is often limiting. Consider the circus elephant. When an elephant is young and small, its keeper fastens a chain from the elephant's ankle to a foot-long stake driven in the ground. No matter how hard the baby elephant pulls, it can't dislodge the stake. As the elephant gets older and larger, it no longer pulls on the stake. It doesn't believe it can dislodge the stake, because that's what it has experienced. In reality, the elephant is confined by an attitude, not a stake, because its great size and strength would easily allow it to pull free.

Likewise, training can overcome limitations that people may have imposed on themselves years ago, when they were different "elephants."

The sign of good management, or leadership, is the ability

to focus a group of individuals on the successful attainment of goals. Management designs the preferred future and then, by either increasing pressure or reducing constraints, moves the group into that future. The training program removes constraints like the chain around the elephant's ankle, and then increases pressure through the specifically assigned objectives, action steps, and deadlines so that new performance levels are reached.

If your company has never designed this kind of training program, the going may be slow. It may be hard to get managers and employees to accept working from the business plan. Still, a journey of 1,000 miles starts with a single step. Instead of letting time pass while you develop and install the perfect program, set up a program that will work now, even if it requires further refinements in the years to come. If suggestions and refinements come from the managers participating in the program, they will develop a genuine sense of ownership of the training program.

Which approach do you think will more genuinely engage a workforce: a program developed by its participants, or an off-the-shelf strategic plan software package that top management completes, prints, and passes out to employees in a neat blue binder? In my experience, it's the home-grown program that

---

Training—Consider Renaming It

To young, highly motivated, ambitious individuals who are looking to advance their careers and make a name for themselves in the company, *training* is a positive term. But it can be demeaning to experienced supervisors and managers who have spent years on the front lines. "Career development" is also a turnoff for people whose careers are well under way.

Even though training is training no matter what it's called, you might want to consider using another term for your program. Since its purpose is to introduce people to the overall business plan and to develop actions that will result in the quickest possible achievement of that plan, a name like *Strategic Plan Implementation Program* may work better.

gets the best results. By developing your own strategic plan training program, you will ensure that everyone in your company understands and is willing to work on the overall business objectives.

Training for Managers

While there isn't any easy way to direct, training makes it easier. By putting your strategic plan down in writing, presenting it during a structured training session, and helping managers develop action steps that implement the plan, you will help managers define their own jobs more precisely and carry out their own responsibilities more effectively, and, in the process, you will make it far likelier that your company will meet its goals and objectives.

Basically, training for managers entails the following:

- Presenting the strategic plan, its overall goals and objectives, and the time frame for accomplishing them.
- Translating the overall goals and objectives into functional and departmental objectives.
- Breaking down functional and departmental objectives into specific action steps and deadlines.
- Assigning those action steps to teams or individuals. After all, individuals accomplish objectives, not departments or companies.

In small companies, this material may all be covered in a single session with all managers. In large companies, each layer of management will conduct its own training, creating a sort of domino effect throughout the organization. The strategic plan itself is developed by the CEO or president and the people who report to him or her. These top managers are responsible for holding the first management training session. They present the plan to their direct reports and work together to translate the plan's goals into functional and departmental goals for each manager. Those managers, in turn, translate goals into specific action steps for their people, and so on, until everyone at every level of the company understands exactly how to implement the strategic plan.

There are two phases to the management training program:

Phase 1. Development of companywide goals, objectives, and deadlines (the *"what* has to be done by *when"* phase)
Phase 2. Administration of the program and processes aspect (the *"who* does *what* by *when"* phase)

Basically, Phase 1 *develops* direction and Phase 2 *gives* direction. Phase 1, the "subject" of the training program, introduces the strategic plan. Every employee—management and nonmanagement—participates in this phase. Management personnel alone complete Phase 2. That is the training techniques, or teaching, package—the structure and methods used to conduct the training and administer the process of directing from the business plan. Phase 2 is what managers are paid to do: direct the activities of the employees assigned to them.

Once managers have been presented with the strategic plan, they work together to break down functional and departmental objectives into specific action steps and responsibilities. As the plan descends through the organization, it gathers more and more detail, until eventually every companywide goal has been broken down into specific tasks and assigned to specific people with concrete deadlines. Presented this way, a strategic plan gathers momentum instead of gathering dust—a real danger for any organization that is content to print up and pass around its plan with no follow-through.

Each time objectives are translated into goals at a lower level of the organizational ladder, a manager who was present at the previous level should be on hand to support the plan. "I don't know why we're doing this, but we're going to do it, damn it" isn't a very strong endorsement of your program. Make sure someone can explain why specific objectives were selected and are being implemented.

All members of the management and supervisory ranks should take part in the training program—even managers who have no direct reports. Even they have to accomplish their own departmental and individual strategic plan–driven objectives, and eventually they may be assigned some staff.

If this process is followed, it will be abundantly clear to each manager in the company just what he or she needs to do to direct employees in the execution of the strategic plan. And once this becomes an annual process, managers will feel more comfortable about directing. What at first glance seemed an intimidating assignment will eventually become second nature!

Phase 1. Translation of Company Objectives

The following sample training session outline addresses a typical contract job shop operation, in which the company makes products to order, rather than for inventory or to meet anticipated demand. The company has set itself two strategic objectives: to increase sales and profits. In Phase 1, management meets to translate those objectives into major action steps that can be assigned to various departments and functions. An all-day meeting devoted to Phase 1 might have as its goal identifying action steps, assigning them to departments or functions, and establishing deadlines. The morning session could introduce the strategic plan and the concept of directing from the plan; the afternoon could be devoted to brainstorming action steps. Remember, starting a program is harder than continuing one. Your company may accomplish this process smoothly or may find that more education and persuasion are needed before everyone can agree and participate.

Stage 1. Translate Company Objectives Into Action Steps With Deadlines

To conduct Phase 1 in your organization, create a fill-in-the-blank worksheet for participants. Across the top of each page, list a goal or objective. Then leave the rest of the page blank so that participants can note action steps as they are debated and discerned. The following sample includes the action steps and substeps developed by the managers of the job shop operation.

Objective 1. Increase sales by 15 percent by year-end.
    Action step 1a.   Review sales targets and adjust upward 15 percent.

Action step 1b. Redesign sales commission program.
Action step 1c. Develop and install new marketing program.

Objective 2. Increase net annual profit by 5 percent.
Action step 2a. Improve productivity in Production by 5 percent.
Action step 2b. Reduce number of unprofitable jobs by 50 percent.

Stage 2. Break Down Major Action Steps Into Specific Substeps

After the action steps are developed, the group works together to identify the substeps required within each of those action steps.

Action step 1a. Review sales targets and adjust upward 15 percent.
Substep 1a-1. Survey industry and similar-size companies for average sales per salesperson.
Substep 1a-2. Review individual salesperson performance against survey data and company standards.
Substep 1a-3. Communicate annual sales targets to sales staff.
Substep 1a-4. Develop and conduct training program for sales staff.

Action step 1b. Redesign sales commission program.
Substep 1b-1. Study alternatives to, and problems with, current sales commission program.
Substep 1b-2. Design, with participation from selected salespeople, new sales commission program.
Substep 1b-3. Present proposed commission program for approval.

Substep 1b-4.   Communicate and install new commission program.

Action step 1c.   Develop and install new marketing program.

Substep 1c-1.   Assign marketing program design and development to outside consulting firm.

Substep 1c-2.   Present proposed marketing program for approval.

Substep 1c-3.   Install new marketing program.

Action step 2a.   Improve productivity in Production by 5 percent.

Substep 2a-1.   Establish study team and develop work-flow diagram for analysis of production procedures.

Substep 2a-2.   Initiate twelve methods improvement ideas to total 5 percent in potential production savings.

Action step 2b.   Reduce number of unprofitable jobs by 50 percent.

Substep 2b-1.   Identify types and causes of unprofitable jobs.

Substep 2b-2.   Recommend procedures to reduce number of unprofitable jobs by 50 percent.

Substep 2b-3.   Install procedures to reduce number of unprofitable jobs by 50 percent.

Stage 3. Assign Substeps to Functions, With Deadlines

After the substeps have been identified, they are assigned to the functions within the company that will be responsible for their accomplishment. In many companies, these substeps would be divided even further; other companies might assign functional responsibilities to subunits such as departments. If either of these procedures is necessary, use the technique shown in Stage 2 to develop additional substeps.

At the end of the meeting, type up this outline and circulate it among the attending managers. List activities, responsible functions, and deadlines. Express deadlines in terms of duration, rather than giving specific calendar dates, as shown in the table on page 72. (Calendar dates are the best method for introducing and assigning objectives to functions and employees.) Don't worry about brevity. It's more important that everyone see all the action steps being addressed and by whom, so that the connection between those steps is apparent.

People need to understand how their own objectives and the objectives of others are related. Distributing a list with all the objectives shows managers that other departments are also participating in the effort to reach the overall, or common, goals. The Portuguese fishermen all understood that the common objective was to fill the hold of the mother ship; until that happened, no one was going home. The skills and jobs of all the fishermen were vitally important to everyone in achieving that goal. Too many managers operate as if the organization were made up of numerous independent companies, each operating as if it were capable of filling the hold of the ship on its own. That's simply not true. Everyone is in this together, and a list of all objectives, action steps, and substeps will make that abundantly clear.

On the other hand, it's important to see each manager and each employee as a kind of independent contractor working on specific projects with clear action steps and deadlines. Every person who takes a job with an organization is really selling his or her independent services in an effort to help that organization reach some objective or higher level of performance. Seeing each person as an independent contractor makes everyone accountable, short-term, for his or her own actions and results as they relate to the company's strategic plan. But this doesn't justify an "every man for himself" attitude. Nip that in the bud by stressing that while individual performance is critical, teamwork is even more important. *Everybody* depends on someone else for input or action.

When everyone has a summary of the goals, action steps, and substeps, it will be easy for each function to highlight the activities that apply to it while understanding the activities that apply to others in the organization. That, in turn, will clarify exactly who is each manager's "internal customer" in the process of working toward the overall objectives.

Assigning Action Steps With Deadlines to the Appropriate Functions

Action Substep	Function(s)	Deadline
1a-1 Survey industry and similar-size companies for average sales per salesperson.	Sales and Human Resources	2 weeks
1a-2. Review individual salesperson performance against survey data and company standards.	Sales	3 weeks
1a-3 Communicate annual sales targets to sales staff.	Sales	4 weeks
1a-4 Develop and conduct training program for sales staff.	Human Resources	5 weeks
1b-1 Study alternatives to, and problems with, current sales commission program.	Human Resources	2 weeks
1b-2 Design, with participation from selected salespeople, new sales commission program.	Sales and Human Resources	4 weeks
1b-3 Present proposed commission program for approval.	Sales and Human Resources	5 weeks
1b-4 Communicate and install new commission program.	Sales	6 weeks
1c-1 Assign marketing program design and development to outside consulting firm.	Marketing	2 weeks
1c-2 Present proposed marketing program for approval.	Marketing	4 weeks

	Action Substep	Function(s)	Deadline
1c-3	Install new marketing program.	Marketing	5 weeks
2a-1	Establish study team and develop work-flow diagram for analysis of production procedures.	Production	3 weeks
2a-2	Initiate twelve methods improvement ideas to total 5 percent in potential production savings.	Production	12 weeks
2b-1	Identify types and causes of unprofitable jobs.	Estimating	3 weeks
2b-2	Recommend procedures to reduce number of unprofitable jobs by 50 percent.	Estimating and Production	5 weeks
2b-3	Install procedures to reduce number of unprofitable jobs by 50 percent.	Estimating and Production	6 weeks

Several of these substeps could be broken down into more-specific action elements. These specific elements would then be assigned to individuals during the Phase 2 training sessions. For example:

> 1b-2   Design, with participation from selected salespeople, new sales commission program.
> 1b-2.1 Select salespeople to take part in commission program redesign.
> 1b-2.2 Conduct sales commission program redesign meetings and develop program.
>
> 1c-1   Assign marketing program design and development to outside consulting firm.
> 1c-1.1 Work with consulting firm to ensure relevant marketing program design.
>
> 2a-1   Establish study team and develop work-flow diagram for analysis of production procedures.

2a-1.1 Select and train team in analysis and developmental techniques.

2a-2   Initiate twelve methods improvement ideas to total 5 percent in potential production savings.

2a-2.1 Select and instruct installation team.

2b-3   Install procedures to reduce number of unprofitable jobs by 50 percent.

2b-3.1 Develop procedures manual to ensure compliance with effort to reduce occurrences of unprofitable jobs.

The two major company objectives, increasing sales by 15 percent and increasing profit by 5 percent, have now been translated into twenty-one functional action steps. This translation from thought to action, and the assignment of those actions to specific parts of the company, will, if managed correctly, result in far more effective and productive direction of employees.

Phase 2. Training in Assigning Action Steps

Phase 2 of the training program instructs managers in how to direct the people who report to them within the framework of overall business objectives.

At first blush, managers may see directing from the business plan as another brick added to their already heavy workload. But in fact, this type of direction is a more efficient, structured way to do their jobs. It asks them to prioritize the work in their function or department in order to aggressively address the company's short- and long-term goals and objectives. Managers participating in the training program need to hear and understand, during the first few moments of the training, that focusing themselves and their people on issues that will bring about real company growth is just as important as their responsibility for day-to-day processing or manufacturing of the company's service or product.

The following training program content list represents the

areas that should be covered in Phase 2 of the managers' program.

Management Program Outline
Strategic Plan Implementation Program

I Introduction to program/process philosophy, goal, and content.
   A. Define strategic plan and the concept of directing from the plan.
   B. Explain how this approach provides focus to entire organization.
   C. Explain importance of defining "reality" and company direction.
   D. Explain importance of converting knowledge into correct action.

II Detail company's specific strategic plan objectives for short and long term.
   A. Explain guiding principles of directing from the business plan.
      1. Need specific, clearly understood objectives when delegating.
      2. Writing down and structuring provides emphasis and focus.
   B. Present content of Phase 1/Stage 1, translation of company objectives into action steps.
      1. Review Objective 1 action steps and reasons supporting them.
      2. Review Objective 2 action steps and reasons supporting them.

III Detail Phase 1/Stage 2; break down major action steps into specific substeps.
   A. Explain how establishing substeps can be an almost never-ending process.
   B. During review with managers, be prepared to incorporate suggestions for further refinement into substeps. Purpose is to instill "ownership" on part of management participants.

IV Detail Phase 1/Stage 3, assignment of substeps to functions, with deadlines.
   A.   Reinforce importance of deadlines for actions: without them, actions are somewhat meaningless, as they may never be performed.
   B.   During review, be prepared to make realistic adjustments to deadlines. Purpose is to instill commitment and "ownership" on part of management participants.
 V Highlight importance of directing all activities using strategic plan objectives as foundation. Everything everyone does should be directed, to some degree, at accomplishing the company's strategic plan objectives.
   A.   All current job content, new job design and creation, and employee selection is related to accomplishing plan objectives.
   B.   Emphasize importance of "progress orientation" versus "process orientation."
   C.   Discuss George Odiorne's claim that employees, at all levels within the organization, understand or are aware of only about 70 percent of what is, or should be, expected of them as contributors.
   D.   Cover concept that companywide and function- or departmentwide teamwork are created through common goal association and commitment.
 VI Discuss issues that appear to be outside directing from the business's strategic plan objectives.
   A.   Discuss providing for day-to-day responsibilities and problem resolution.
   B.   Discuss internal customer aspect and how this ties into the overall effort.
VII Present importance and relevance of measurement in company operations.
   A.   Discuss need for milestones and deadlines, along with degree of flexibility to be allowed in changing or adjusting those times.
   B.   Explain that goals are neither ceilings nor minimums.
   C.   Outline how program becomes basis for performance expectations and standards, for individual employees and entire company.

VIII Present next steps in program/process development and administration.
  A. Explain nonmanagement training program and managers' roles in that program.
    1. Managers have to promote commitment to the program/process and instill confidence that it is necessary, practical, and workable.
    2. Managers have to become adept at presentation skills and at addressing and leading group discussions.
    3. Managers have to learn to respond confidently to employee concerns and questions about their roles in the process and the consequences of their performance levels.
    4. Managers have to become expert at directing the mechanics of the program/process.
  B. Discuss development, by managers, of individual employee or job classification goals, milestones, and deadlines.
    1. Managers have to study current design of jobs and, if necessary, redesign jobs that do not fit company objectives and focus.
    2. Managers have to assign objectives and deadlines to individual employees or groups of employees by job classification.
    3. Managers have to continually review, measure, and monitor performance of individuals in their ongoing progress toward meeting objectives.
    4. Managers have to react to performance variations, on the part of their employees and themselves, and take whatever action is necessary.
  C. Explain that this program/process will be performed and refined on an annual basis. It will become "the way we do things around here."

Section VIII. Where Managers Learn the Basics of Direction

Section VIII of the outline is where the rubber meets the road—where managers learn about and begin to prepare for their role in directing employees in meeting the company's overall short- and long-term objectives.

Many managers are weak in giving direction. That's because they are often selected not for their directing skills but for their expertise in the long-standing processes of their function or area. As a result, they can easily process the hour-by-hour or day-by-day work through their departments, work that may have little to do with overall strategic objectives. But they may not want to go where they've never been or do what they've never done—both of which are required if they are to become better managers.

Direction is not a difficult skill to develop, and a person doesn't need to be an expert to get the desired results. While expertise helps, direction mostly takes attention, diligence, attitude, and clear communication. The right kinds of forms and reports for initiating, recording, and following up on activities are also important. When they are consistently used, they supply the glue that holds everything together.

Section VIII of the management training program outline details the skills needed, how to apply them in delegating individual objectives, and the forms or reports that support those actions.

❑ *Item B1.* Clear job descriptions are the basis for developing goals, milestones, and deadlines. Managers must continually review the tasks they and their employees perform to make sure that every task assigned and performed supports the primary and secondary, or long- and short-term, objectives of the company. While a long-term objective like "improve profits by 5 percent" may not change for a year, the short-term objectives required to meet that objective change often. Middle managers need to be sure that those short-term objectives are addressed in daily, on-the-job activities.

Use Exhibit 5-1 to review job content and assign substeps or individual objectives with milestones and deadlines. It is also useful for assigning objectives to job classifications or groups of employees. It's an essential communication tool for transmitting companywide objectives to employees during group or one-on-one meetings.

Exhibit 5-1. Sample job description with objectives.

Job Description and Objectives

Position title: Manager, Estimating
Reports to: President
Date: xx/xx/xx

General Responsibilities

Direct and coordinate all Estimating activities for company. Formulate and administer all policies and procedures for function. Supervise Estimating personnel and evaluate individual performance. Coordinate with and advise other departments. Perform duties of estimator on many occasions.

Specific Objectives		Deadline
Substep 2b-1	Identify types and causes of unprofitable jobs.	xx/xx/xx
Substep 2b-2	Recommend procedures to reduce number of unprofitable jobs by 50 percent (with Production)	xx/xx/xx
Substep 2b-3	Install procedures to reduce number of unprofitable jobs by 50 percent (with Production)	xx/xx/xx

Assigned to: _____   Assigned by: _____

Read & Understood: _____ (signature)

During this stage of the training, managers should practice developing job descriptions and assigning initial substeps and time frames. Practice gives managers a head start when they begin to train to deal with their own employees in the subsequent sessions or meetings, whether they are with managers or nonmanagers.

❑ *Item B2.* This is not as simple as it seems. The translation of overall strategic business objectives has to be coordinated with the different functions and departments that will tackle them. The milestones and deadlines for all substeps must also be linked. This requires close and continual follow-through by upper-level managers who are assigning objectives.

Assigning objectives to groups of employees within the same job classification means assigning the objective or objectives to the person responsible for the respective group. In other words, the objective is assigned to one person, who uses supervision and leadership to see it to completion through the work of his or her employees. Exhibit 5-2, the objective status report, can be used to record and report individual and group progress. Post the form to remind everyone in the departments of the effort and deadline.

❑ *Item B3.* To accomplish a goal, progress must be monitored continually at predetermined interim dates, not when events or milestones occur. Waiting for something to occur before you measure progress may cause you to be continually late and fail to meet your objectives. Every functional and individual objective is related. Think of a line of cars hitting their brakes one after another and you'll have an idea of the slowdown created when deadlines in just one area start to slip. Most deadlines should have some cushion built into them to allow for the unexpected, but once time targets are set, they should become a pledge. Don't leave space for an "adjusted" date on your status report form. Stick with a completion date only. Employees have to make commitments that they live up to and that others can depend on. That's why these dates are called deadlines.

❑ *Item B4.* If directing from the overall business plan is to become a common practice in an organization, short- and long-term objectives must be seen as part of everyone's job. These

Exhibit 5-2. Sample objective status report.

Objective Status Report

Objective:	1. Increase sales by 15 percent by year-end.
Action Step:	1a. Review sales targets and adjust upward 15 percent.
Substep:	1a-1. Survey industry and similar-size companies for average sales per salesperson.

Steps	Assigned to	Deadline	Status
Determine proper survey	TW & JO	xx/xx/xx	Completed; selected PII survey
Gather survey data	TW & JO	xx/xx/xx	In process
Format data for report	TW & JO	xx/xx/xx	—
Present data with summary	TW	xx/xx/xx	—

COMMENTS: _____

Reported by: AM

Date: xx/xx/xx

tasks are not extras, or add-ons to the "normal" job. This means that failure to accomplish those tasks is failure to perform. If the objective and the time allowed for it were realistic, then the fault lies with the unexpected event or the employee. Whatever the cause, it is the manager's job to deal with the problem.

Direction and the Job Audit

To obtain the greatest benefit from directing from the business plan, job activities and responsibilities need to be reviewed annually. Management and key nonmanagement personnel should go over the primary and secondary tasks required in every one of the operation's jobs, seeking ways to:

- ❑ Remove unnecessary activities.
- ❑ Focus on tasks that need more attention.
- ❑ Redesign jobs that need redesigning.
- ❑ Incorporate any short- or long-term company objectives.

Reviewing tasks and objectives and packaging them into efficient jobs, communicating the subsequent activities to employees, and training those employees in the acceptable levels of performance is the most basic element of management. It is essential that managers direct based on audited job content and design. If this aspect of their management is flawed or incomplete, their training and directing of employees will also be flawed or incomplete.

Unfortunately, many managers are reluctant to create or revise job descriptions, even though these descriptions list the duties and responsibilities of each person whose performance and expense to the company they are held accountable for. Some managers believe that descriptions will restrict the activities of their people—but what they mean is that they don't want to take the time or make the effort to draft them, especially if the duties of their employees will change soon.

When activities are in a fluid state, descriptions are even more important. Spelling out what has to be done, outlining hiring requirements, and determining pay levels are all very definite management responsibilities. Unless job content is reviewed regularly, duties and responsibilities will be only guessed at or ignored.

While descriptions are important, it is the *process* of reviewing job tasks on a broad scale that reveals tasks that are duplicated, inefficient, overlapping, or just plain unnecessary. The results of this exercise, when formalized in job descriptions or process sheets, are essential to directing and redirecting the workforce.

Objectives: Ceilings or Minimums?

When strategic plan–based direction is installed in a company, managers and employees alike wonder whether the objectives they are asked to meet are ceilings or minimums. Is accomplishing your set of objectives considered above-average performance, or is it the minimum required to earn a satisfactory rating? If employees make objectives early, will the boss assign new ones or wait until next year's strategic plan? Will objectives be ratcheted up to ever tougher levels if they are met ahead of schedule, or will they be made easier if employees continually come up short but are otherwise solid performers? The answers depend on the difficulty of the goals, objectives, milestones, and deadlines. If the targets require aggressive and time-consuming efforts, they might be seen as ceilings and their accomplishment regarded as grounds for commendation. If they are easy to meet, they should be seen as minimums.

A manager's or employee's workload is another factor. While everything a person does should be directly related to the company's overall business plan, non-goal-related tasks will always be necessary to operate the department or work area, whether it's delivering parts, fixing equipment, or dealing with

---

Leave Time for Local Objectives

While the management training will largely focus on strategic plan objectives, be sure to leave time to develop "local," or specific, objectives that address improvements to the effectiveness of the respective departments or functions. Replacing a worn office chair, for example, may improve someone's effectiveness, and therefore addresses a company strategic plan objective. But this kind of objective needs to be initiated by a local manager or supervisor, not top management. Leave some time in your agenda to develop and discuss this kind of objective, too.

computer problems. If the job is greatly affected by this type of activity, then the accomplishment of any additional goals may require significant effort.

I think the issue of ceilings or minimums is really a red herring that distracts from the very point of managing employee direction from the strategic plan. Setting objectives and goals in the context of the strategic or business plan is a matter of setting direction, not identifying a finish line. It is an attempt to overcome the tendency of an organization or individual to lose sight of the important and common direction of the company. Objectives guide people as a compass guides a hiker. A compass tells us the direction in which we're traveling, not when we'll get there. While solid and aggressive application of goals, objectives, and deadlines will make a company more competitive, there will never be a finish line. The question of when to reestablish individuals' goals is secondary to the responsibility of providing ongoing focus and direction to those individuals through goals.

Directing from a business plan is like driving from New York to New Orleans. You can tell someone to start driving, or you can supply a map marked with the shortest route. The driver given the map does not need any training in the usual sense; you haven't added any significant or unusual skills to the assignment. You just have to take a little more time to present and explain the route markings to that driver. Directing from the business's strategic plan is similar. Don't make more of it than it really is. If your organization's managers cannot grasp and apply this direction process, then it's time to start looking for managers who can.

CHAPTER 6

Training Nonmanagement Personnel

The whole point of directing from the business plan is to create a common energy force within the organization that will propel the company toward its important objectives. In many companies, this kind of energy already exists among top management. It can be spread throughout the organization by training everyone in the goals and objectives of the strategic plan and the action steps that will help accomplish those goals. With a strategic plan implementation program installed at every level of the company, middle managers, first-line supervisors and managers, and nonmanagement personnel can contribute their personal energy to the common energy force.

Once that energy force has been created, it has to be contained and directed. The direction is provided by the managers through the instruction and training they have received and through their day-to-day application of that information on the job.

Direction also takes place through training for nonmanagement personnel. This training is designed to tell them about directing from the business plan and to explain their part in the overall effort. It also highlights the expectations that the organization has set for itself through its management and nonmanagement employees. All of this should provide the basis for that energy force.

Before you can train nonmanagement personnel, you need to explain why the company is shifting to a new direction process. You'll have to make it clear that training is more than just a management program—it is a technique for focusing the entire organization on its goals. All employees need to understand that their behavior is expected to contribute significantly to the outcome.

If they see training as little more than an effort to tell them what management is working on this year, they will tend to sit back and watch the game. If the company is to make all the progress it can in the shortest time possible, you have to bring the employees down from the grandstands and onto the playing field. It's like a tug-of-war: The more people you have on your end of the rope, the better your chances of winning.

Positioning the Training Program

Just as the military trains its nonleadership personnel in the why and how behind the duties and roles they are expected to fulfill, your nonmanagement personnel need to understand the why and how behind their own assignments and responsibilities.

Employees need to know why the company wants to improve profit, reduce costs, or introduce a new product every quarter. Employees who know that the company's survival depends on the accomplishment of an objective will dedicate themselves to meeting the challenge. Employees at every level need to know that the objectives they are being asked to work on have real significance and weren't devised just to make their bosses look good.

This kind of knowledge will come from the training program, but first you need to explain why you're asking employees to participate. For the program to be effective, people need to understand its purpose. It's never enough to say, "This is good for you and the organization." In fact, statements like that will cause people to resist or ignore the program before it ever gets going. Tell your employees the philosophy behind the purpose and goal of the program. Tell them that it will explain the company's strategic plan and help them understand their role in the big picture.

If your company has been having difficulty achieving its strategic objectives, this new approach to direction will be easy to justify. Basically, it's a cure for a very big problem. If your small, easy-to-manage company has successfully met its objectives in the past but is now on the verge of fast growth, pitch the training program as prevention. Explain that it will help the company continue to meet its goals as objectives become more subtle and the number of employees increases. Let the employees know that the training program will keep everyone "in the loop" so that they do not have to wonder where the company is going.

Above all, stress that the training program is only the opening salvo in a new approach to your business. Effective immediately, more will be expected of everyone in the organization. To prove it, you will be sharing information about the company that people have not heard before. That's because you want people to understand how their own work fits into the overall picture, and how they are expected to contribute to overall company objectives as well as day-to-day, short-term departmental responsibilities.

Managers are used to meeting high expectations. They know that they are responsible for getting things done, on time, through others. That's not true of nonmanagement folks. The typical employee feels that he or she is paid to apply a certain level of effort, over a predetermined span of time, in a manner dictated by the written procedures for the job or a supervisor's instructions. That often means performing structured tasks that help the company produce its products or services.

Your company needs people to do more than just perform those tasks if it is to succeed. It also needs input on ways to improve the operation or to meet objectives in all aspects of the business. You can tweak your selection process and start hiring people who are ready and willing to contribute new ideas and meet higher expectations, but your current employees will need to be nudged in this direction. You can urge them along by demonstrating how management is shifting its attitude and changing its practices.

First, you need to convince employees that management believes that everyone truly can function at this higher level of involvement. Second, you need to develop, install, and operate a structured system that allows employee suggestions to surface and be reviewed. Together, these steps indicate greater expectations for employees. Management says that it believes that employees have far greater contributions to make, and that it is putting procedures in place to allow those contributions.

Simply telling employees that they should contribute more will not change their behavior. You need to tell them which areas of the business need improvement. You have to give very specific goals for increasing productivity, profit, or sales so that they understand what you mean by improvement or change. And you have to establish credibility by linking the information and expectations to the employees' current and future job situation.

Most nonmanagement employees smile or shiver when they are told that management would appreciate and even welcome ideas on how to make the operation or company more productive and competitive. Generally, employees respond in one of three ways. Some think that coming up with improvements is what management is paid for. Some suspect an effort to eliminate jobs, perhaps their own. Others see an opportunity to reveal the many ideas that they have been harboring, but thought that management didn't really want to hear. All three of these reactions have to be addressed and techniques applied that bring everyone around to the common goals of greater involvement, participation, contribution, and productivity. And that's what the nonmanagement version of the strategic plan implementation program can do.

People have different reactions to this type of program and process. As in many situations, a bell-shaped curve will apply. People on one end of the curve will think the concepts are the greatest; folks on the other end will think they are garbage. The majority in the middle will tolerate the program or won't care one way or the other.

The odds are that you won't get a standing ovation when you introduce or conduct the training. Your basic message is that there is room for improvement in the manner in which time is being spent in the organization. The only thing that will convince employees that this training is a good idea will be seeing that it works, and even then you won't get that ovation.

People are hired and paid to achieve certain objectives. The clearer those objectives are, the more likely people are to do the right things and do them right the first time, and the faster they can move on to the next objective. Doing more of the right things faster and less expensively is one way to beat other companies and stay in business. People who won't go along with this basic thinking either don't get it or don't want to work very hard. In either case, you don't need them on your payroll. And the sooner you find this out and do something about it, the more profitable things will be for you and your company.

Phase 1. Sharing the Strategic Plan With Employees

Training for nonmanagement employees, like training for managers, is divided into two phases. Phase 1, which presents the strategic plan, is essentially identical for managers and nonmanagement employees. (To organize the program, follow the outlines in Chapter 5.) Everyone needs to understand the rationale behind the strategic plan and the goals and objectives the company is striving to achieve. Of course, you may want to omit objectives that require some level of confidentiality, such as mergers or acquisitions or new product research. News of these undertakings may never get out of the boardroom, especially if they are being handled by people outside of the company, and so may never reach the average employee or manager. But no matter how the content is altered for employees, your goal is to establish common ground throughout the organization.

As well as introducing company objectives, Phase 1 solicits feedback from employees. As you lead them through the strategic plan, let them know that their ideas are welcomed. Set it up like this:

> I know what you're thinking—this is management's job. But we are asking you to help from now on. We need your ideas. After all, the best ideas come from people who are

actually doing the job. That's because people who do the job are experts on the best way to do it. We need ideas in order to grow our business by becoming more competitive and more efficient, and selling our products and services at a better price. If you come up with a productivity improvement, we will be more likely to grow as a company.

Reassure people that their ideas are truly welcome. If you are introducing a program to reward employees for their ideas, explain it here. Especially if employees have had their ideas rejected in the past, you will need to underscore the new openness to feedback and suggestions.

After participants learn the company's key objectives, tell them the purposes behind them. Let them know, for example, that increasing sales by 15 percent will expand the business and thereby provide job growth and security for employees, and that increasing profits by 5 percent will allow the company to upgrade its technology and contribute more to the profit-sharing or 401(k) plan.

Next, show participants how managers have translated key objectives into action steps. Allow plenty of time for this segment so that everyone understands the process of developing the activities needed to support the concepts. Next, show them how the substeps were identified, and how they were assigned to specific functions or departments. Information on the deadlines assigned for those objectives in the respective areas follows.

Leave time for brainstorming. As in the management training sessions, there should be room for employees to contribute their own ideas about how to translate objectives into departmental activities. When they see how their jobs fit into the overall purpose and direction of the company, employees will feel more confident about proposing new ideas and processes. By welcoming those ideas in the very first training session, you will set the tone for future idea exchanges.

Set aside time for a question-and-answer session, too. In most situations, it is a good idea to develop a half dozen or so key questions and answers that deal with the basic philosophies and theories of the program and process. Some examples of those types of questions, and possible answers, are the following:

❏ *Why is the company doing this?* Top management wants to make sure that the goals and objectives the company needs to meet are being addressed as part of every employee's job. It is important that we all understand that each of us is vital to the ongoing competitiveness and growth of this business. If we establish a close association between our strategic plan and each person in the company, success should come more quickly because all our everyday efforts will be more productive and focused.

❏ *How will we be evaluated against these objectives?* If you make your individual objectives, even if the company fails to reach its two or three overall key objectives, you will receive credit for your performance. In the long term, however, the company's failure may indirectly affect you. If the company achieves its key objectives and you as an individual fail to make your targets, your performance review will show that failure.

❏ *Will this affect my current workload?* That depends. In most cases this effort will provide better direction and focus to your daily activities. Therefore, your workload should not be increased. Also, you may be performing some activities that do not contribute as much as they used to, considering our new objectives. It will be your manager's responsibility to study the content of jobs to see if this applies. This is not a push to get more out of people; it is designed to make us all more productive for the sake of the business and for ourselves.

❏ *What if the company has to change or add objectives in mid-year?* We may have to shift priorities to account for some unforeseen issues or opportunities, but we do this now. We do not want to become so attached to objectives set in the past that we lose out on opportunities in the future. This is not, however, likely to happen, as the key objectives generally will not be the type that change in a short time span.

❏ *Is every employee affected by this program?* In theory, everyone should be. Each and every job in this organization was created and filled because the tasks included in that position were needed in order to service customers, support sales, and generate profit. Whether you will be assigned individual objectives depends on your job classification. But all of us will, either directly or indirectly, be working to accomplish some part or parts of the key goals.

❑ *If, after the first try, this process doesn't work, will the company continue it?* This is not some new management fad. It is simply a better and more focused way to manage our daily activities. If it accomplishes only 25 percent of what it should on the first try, we will still all be better off. We will continue to operate this way because we cannot afford to operate any other way.

These types of questions and answers, along with handouts covering the action steps and substeps with deadlines, should be distributed to participants.

Phase 2. Receiving and Performing Action-Step Assignments

While Phase 1 informs employees of the overall business direction, explains the company's new expectations, and begins to secure commitment to meeting company targets, Phase 2 is oriented toward the individual.

Directing the individual nonmanagement employee in his or her day-to-day job is best accomplished when the employee understands the connection between that job and the department and company as a whole. An awareness that each individual is a vital part of everything that is eventually produced by the organization is critical to a manager's effectiveness. Managers who do not understand or believe this tend to have lower standards and expectations of their people and, as a result, are less productive at managing.

These managers are compulsive people managers, rather than task managers. They often see their job as solving trait-related problems. If an employee fails to deal with the details of an assignment, with the result that the overall task is not done properly, some managers will attempt to train the person to become more detail-minded. But it's impossible to define a detail in terms that everyone, or at least the manager and the specific employee, will agree on.

What the manager can do, however, is define the components of the task in a way that clarifies how he or she want things done. These elements are no longer details left up to the person performing the job; instead, they become required steps. The result is a procedure, a packaged series of tasks that are clear to everyone. Now the manager has objective job elements to be used in the direction of the employee, rather than subjective personal traits like "detailedness."

As Chapter 4 made clear, the main reason managers have trouble getting the results they want from the people they supervise is that not all of the desired results are clearly defined in advance of the performance. Too many managers practice "ambush-style" direction, in which they explain what they really expected after someone has completed the job according to the original directions.

There are only two reasons why people don't do things that are expected of them and have been made clear to them: Either they can't, or they won't. If they can't because they have not been properly trained, then it's your responsibility to train them. If they have been trained and still can't do the job, then it's your responsibility to replace them because, in all likelihood, they will never be able to do the job. You should also replace anyone who has received thorough direction and can do the job, but simply won't.

Phase 2 of the training program should be designed to ensure that nonmanagement employees understand how the company objectives explained in Phase 1 will be defined in terms of direction and action steps in their department and job classification. This part of the training will result in direction that is specific to either the individual or the job classification, depending on the type of business, operation, department, or job.

In a flexible organization in which nonmanagement employees make a considerable number of hour-to-hour or day-to-day decisions, individual goals, objectives, milestones, and deadlines may apply down to the very last person. If these people are receiving a minimal amount of direct supervision, you need to make sure that what direction they get is the best possible. These people really need to know and understand what is expected of them and how and where to focus their energies.

They need to make decisions about what to do next or how to handle a certain situation within the framework of the business plan. They need to be consistent, and their efforts need to be linked with the efforts and focus of others.

In a more rigidly structured organization, with narrowly defined jobs and close supervision of hour-by-hour tasks, the development of objectives for individuals may not be practical or possible. But that doesn't mean that objectives from the business plan cannot filter down to the lowest levels in the company. It just means that those objectives, milestones, and deadlines may have to be developed for each job classification instead of each individual employee. Everyone in the same job classification, or with the same job title, will then understand the collective objectives of that organizational role.

When managers work from objectives—when they are continually outlining or redesigning procedures and jobs that are their responsibility—there is always a need to retrain people. This kind of environment requires people to become multi-skilled and flexible in their roles—something that most nonmanagement professionals regard as risky. They would rather be specialists, staying up to date with a particular trade or profession. While technicians, assemblers, and distribution personnel and other nonprofessionals are less concerned about moving out of their current jobs, they are still reluctant to retrain. Their worry is that they may not be able to learn new responsibilities at a rate that meets changing company standards.

For both of these groups, you need to assure people that flexibility and retraining are not threats. Phase 2 of the nonmanagement training program explains how the organization will be giving direction in the future. It needs to explain that jobs and procedures may be redesigned as a result of changes in technology, product or service, or customer demands. While many nonmanagement people seek stability in what they do, that attitude has to be realigned with the reality that jobs and processes have to be managed in a manner that allows for, and in some instances creates, change.

Individuals who are anticipating changes in their environment will be much better prepared for those changes if they know that they are necessary. The best way to develop stability in a job or career is to adapt to and be capable of functioning within unstable situations. The core message of this second phase of the training should be, "Expect anything, and here is how it will be communicated to you, and this is how we should all react." This is an important attitude to develop in managers and employees alike. Don't fall into the trap of thinking that as long as the equipment or operation remains the same from year to year, the management and issues remain the same. They don't!

Even if you are managing a strongly traditional business whose machinery or product has changed little, your customers' expectations may have shifted. The competition probably has changed the way they operate. Your employees may be following procedures that are outdated or inefficient, or they (and you) may have become complacent and casual in their treatment of customers or work. That's why it is important to conduct at least a yearly review and initiative addressed at the focus and direction of all employees.

Implementing Phase 2

When you conduct Phase 2, make the point that you are moving from the collective stage to the individual stage. Explain that the purpose of the material to follow is to prepare individuals for one-on-one or job classification group meetings with their managers. It will also help them understand how to best operate under a process that now includes specific short-term objectives based on the company's overall business plan.

Nonmanagement Program Outline
Strategic Plan Implementation Program

I Explain that the purpose of this phase is to prepare participants for assignment and successful performance of individual or group objectives.

II Make the following points and provide for discussion on each.
   A. The purpose of the process is to focus daily efforts on

selected key business objectives and to turn that and other knowledge into action.

B. The process will provide for clearer identification of performance expectations for everyone.

C. The process does not mean added work. Instead, it means better direction in doing those things that are vital to the company as a whole, and improved use of employee time.

D. Some objectives may require that individuals become part of a specific team that has responsibility for accomplishing an objective or objectives.

E. Progress will be audited and reported on schedules to be determined in each function or department.

F. Individuals and teams should give notice of deadline slippage or other problems at the earliest possible time. Management needs to know so that appropriate action can be taken. Discuss the impact on others when deadlines slip.

G. The company will become much more "measurement-based" than in the past. (*Allow question-and-answer period.*)

III Conduct individual or group assignment of objectives and deadlines.

Who Conducts These Sessions and How?

The size of the company or organization determines who conducts these sessions with nonmanagement personnel and how they are conducted. Companies with fifty or fewer nonmanagement employees may be able to reach everyone in a single session conducted by a member or members of the top management team. In this meeting, participants could receive all of the instruction down to the actual assignment of objectives, which would be conducted by their respective first-level managers or supervisors, one on one or with the group job classifications, a few days after the training.

In larger organizations, first-level managers can conduct training for the people reporting to them. One-on-one and group

Exhibit 6-1. Form for tracking a department's progress toward its goals.

Function/Department: Production

Specific Action Steps	Assigned To	Start Date	Status	Finish Date
Action Step 2a. Improve productivity in Production by 5 percent. Substep 2a-1: Establish study team and develop work-flow diagram for analysis of production procedures.	Management			
Substep 2a-2. Initiate twelve methods improvement ideas to total 5 percent in potential production savings.	Study Team			
Action Step 2b. Reduce number of unprofitable jobs by 50 percent. Substep 2b-1. Identify types and causes of unprofitable jobs.	Study Team			
Substep 2b-2. Recommend procedures to reduce number of unprofitable jobs by 50 percent.	Study Team			
Substep 2b-3. Install procedures to reduce number of unprofitable jobs by 50 percent.	Management and Study Team			

assignments can be made during those sessions, depending on the number of participants and the number of different job types represented.

Generally speaking, the broader portion of the training program can be done in groups of any size, as participation and questions are usually limited. Assigning objectives should be conducted at the most basic, and lowest, levels in the organization.

Measuring Progress

Once substeps have been assigned, progress toward strategic plan objectives needs to be measured. Top management needs to continually review the status of the action steps and substeps and maintain a current feel for the overall performance of management in achieving those objectives. It is a simple enough task to create a report that can be updated through computers throughout the company. Such a report would list every objective, action step, substep, deadline, milestone, and responsible manager or nonmanager. With weekly status input, anyone in the organization, not just top management, can review progress and enter status information.

Exhibit 6-1, on page 97, shows a form designed to help a production department track progress toward its goals. A form like this provides all the information needed to monitor and measure the direction program, while placing every assignment in full view of anyone who might need to trace elements of associated objectives. Without this type of report, it is difficult to ensure quick and effective overall management, and measurement, of the process. And measurement is an essential part of evaluation, the third of the Four Elements of Successful Management.

PART THREE
Evaluate

Evaluation is intimidating. Often, managers are too busy to keep up with what people are doing and how well they are doing it. And when managers *don't* know what their people are doing, they can't evaluate accurately. As a result, they feel unable to support their impressions or comments about performance—and so they avoid the task.

But when selection and direction are done properly, evaluation becomes a logical, easy-to-implement process. If you know what your people are supposed to do and have assigned each of them specific tasks, responsibilities, and objectives with deadlines, then you have criteria against which to measure that individual's performance. In this situation, evaluation becomes a simple matter of determining whether or not a person has met those goals, and how well.

Managers often assume that if they select good people and direct them in what is expected, things will get done. They're right. Things *will* get done, but how well they will get done and how long they will take are uncertain. Evaluation lets you determine how well something was done and whether it was done on time. In a sense, evaluation is like a traffic cop. You can post all the speed limit signs in the world, but they will be ignored unless people know that infractions will be discovered and fined.

This sounds logical, but it's surprising how many managers postpone evaluation again and again while they focus on more pressing but ultimately less important duties. When evaluation is postponed, deadlines also slip, because employees begin to feel that timeliness and quality are not important. When performance slips, more responsibilities shift to the manager—who thus has even less time to direct and evaluate employees.

This section covers the elements of the successful evaluation program. It will help you prepare for and conduct an effective evaluation meeting that will help you determine not just an employee's past performance, but also what the employee's future role in the company should be.

And that's the goal of the evaluation process: to make sure that the talents of your employees are utilized in a way that benefits you, the employee, and the company.

CHAPTER 7

Knowing What to Evaluate

Effective managers may have startlingly different styles of evaluating employee performance, but they share a common trait: They know what to evaluate. They know that in order for management to be effective or outstanding, it must be built around what an organization, function, department, team, or individual has to accomplish. What you want to get done determines the kind of people you select to fill your jobs. What you want to get done determines the design of those jobs and therefore the direction you give the people you select. What you want to get done should also determine how you evaluate employees. Basically, you need to evaluate *what* is getting done, not *who* is doing it.

When is also important. Every manager and supervisor should evaluate the activities of every subordinate every single day. This doesn't mean that managers have to hover over people. It does mean that they should be prepared to step into any performance or behavioral situation that is interfering with the output, goals, efficiencies, and safety of the company, operation, function, department, or other employees. This is what managers are paid to do, and any manager who does not understand, does not agree, or is too timid or unsure to perform these responsibilities is not doing his or her job.

Performance evaluation can be the most productive aspect of management, or the most destructive. A manager who does nothing else well but gets the required results through people will probably have a great and successful career. And even a knowledgeable manager won't last long if he or she can't get his or her employees to get things done correctly or on time. That's why the managers of sports teams get fired before the players. Managers are paid for the results they get from the team, not for how much they know about the game. An expert on the technical aspects of a game may be great at color commentary, but even networks want someone with a winning record. So if you want to manage, you had better get this part of the job down to a science—which it can almost be reduced to if the proper strategy is in place within the organization.

The basic concepts and principles of performance evaluation are the same whether they are applied to management or nonmanagement personnel. The essence of performance evaluation strategy is to:

- ❏ Determine a core set of responsibilities and specific action steps or objectives, related to the organization's overall business goal, that are to be performed by an individual within a specified time frame.
- ❏ Communicate these responsibilities, action steps, and objectives to the employee so that the employee knows exactly the criteria against which his or her performance will be measured and when completion is expected.
- ❏ Review the employee's progress regularly or as required based on performance or behavior.

The essence of performance evaluation, in other words, is direction. When direction is clear, you will have the criteria you need to evaluate performance using the following steps:

- ❏ Schedule an annual performance evaluation meeting with each employee.
- ❏ Prepare for each meeting by gathering information and statistics on the person's performance and reflecting on it. Next, determine specific performance items to discuss during the meeting. Ask the employee to evaluate his or her own performance so that the two of you can use the meeting to discuss the differences between your perceptions.

❏ Hold the meeting and compare and discuss your two evaluations. Where the two of you differ is where you should begin to talk!

The more time you can devote to preparing for the meeting, the more productive the meeting will be. Keep in mind that the ultimate goal of the meeting and the entire evaluation process is more than just accurately measuring performance. The real objective is to apply that information in a way that results in improved further utilization of the employee—generally through setting new objectives that allow the employee to use his or her skills in the most beneficial way.

Why Measuring Performance Is Important

Business is measurement. We measure profits, costs, sales, quality, market share, and progress against all sorts of objectives and goals. All of these measurements are really prima facie evidence of employee performance at all levels of the company.

Some people argue that only top management, which directs others toward the performance needed or desired, should be held accountable for those types of numbers. They also hold that when performance is under par, it is top management's responsibility to recognize and fix it. These people believe that top managers are the only people who should continually evaluate and react to correct inadequate results.

The reality is that *everyone* in an organization is accountable for big-ticket items like profits or sales. Every person in the organization can be evaluated in terms of these items, either directly or by tracking a series of related activities. For example, an operation might invest in state-of-the-art equipment and tools in order to improve productivity. When productivity doesn't improve, management may eventually find that the problem lies in the manner in which the employees are using the equipment and tools. Good managers know that the equipment and tools are only as productive as the people using them.

It's not enough to simply evaluate people on things like "ability to get along with others." Managers must measure employee performance using real issues like profit and productivity—they should be measured not on how hard they try or on how well they fit in, but on the results they produce.

In a sense, a manager is a "resulter"—someone who is responsible for results produced by others. One way to ensure that you get those results is to think of performance appraisal or evaluation as a continual process of purchasing services from employees. Each day you evaluate what you are getting for the money you are spending on payroll. If you aren't getting what you want, but you continue to evaluate in the same manner, then it's your fault, not your employees'.

Look at every employee as if he or she were an independent contractor whose services, if they fail to provide immediate results, need to be redirected or terminated. Not only is this the only cost-effective way to manage, but it is the only way to ensure that overall performance standards will continue to rise rather than fall or slip. Removing the poor performers raises the average performance level throughout an organization; condoning poor performance tends to lower output levels. Experience shows that having and maintaining high standards of performance causes the right employees to be proud of both the company and themselves, which, in turn, leads to greater productivity. This is basic management theory. You can find it as far back in history as 42 B.C., when the ancient Roman mime Publilius Syrus wrote, "He hurts the good who spares the bad."

There is no such thing as a job that cannot be measured or evaluated. The very purpose of a job is to accomplish some result. If the result can be defined, then the performance expectations can be expressed in similar terms. If the performance cannot be measured, it may be because there are no real job goals or objectives and therefore there is no real job. But many times even the lack of a job to measure against doesn't stop some managers from plunging ahead with the evaluation process or meeting. That's when evaluation comes to resemble the Sheriff-and-Posse Strategy.

The Sheriff-and-Posse Strategy

Remember those Western movies in which the sheriff assembled a posse to go after the bad guys? The sheriff's toughest task was keeping the posse together through the long days and nights of the chase. When following a trail grew boring and the sheriff had little to evaluate, he had to spend his time bolstering the morale of his frustrated men. Without some "little victories" to celebrate, the sheriff had to draw on his credibility and salesmanship to keep his staff together. He had to do whatever it took to keep posse members from dropping out, heading back to town, and telling the town's population that the sheriff didn't know what he was doing.

When there aren't any real tasks or objectives to evaluate, managers begin to evaluate people and the work or personal habits of those people—issues that take managers into areas that cannot be dealt with effectively. A manager who doesn't look first at specific, task-oriented results often begins evaluating what a person seems capable of doing instead of what he or she has been doing. Skipping results and going to capabilities means that the evaluation meeting becomes vague and unproductive. If the supervisor or manager spends too much time on the things that the employee feels she or he can or should be doing, that supervisor or manager may end up advising the person in career development, instead of conducting an evaluation of past performance. That manager is simply trying to keep his or her posse together in case there is some activity later on down the trail.

For example, the manager may tell the employee that he or she is performing well and that in a short time things will begin to happen that will present opportunities to that employee. The employee is now looking past the immediate job at some vague possibility in the future. Unrealistic expectations begin to be formed, and the manager has a disgruntled employee who will have to be dealt with sooner or later if no new responsibilities materialize.

But this is not the only danger that arises from an unfocused evaluation meeting. Charges of discrimination are far more serious, and they are a definite possibility in any meeting that focuses on personality or personal issues instead of specific job tasks or elements. Because appraisal meetings of this type often end with little or no changes in the employee's job status other than the possibility of a token pay increase, the employee may feel that he or she has been waltzed around in circles. Upon recalling the conversation later, the person may begin to read into certain statements a meaning that was not intended.

For example, a manager who was conducting a rather casual, off-the-cuff performance review with a recently divorced female employee who had sole custody of her young daughter did not take the time to develop specific performance items for discussion. Instead, he tried a less structured approach, hoping to develop a closer understanding of the employee's situation by asking her about the new child-care problems she must be facing. Difficulties regarding travel and extended workdays came up. The meeting ended with some comments about keeping up the good work. A few days later, the employee asked the manager if she was being passed over for additional responsibilities because her personal life would get in the way. The manager tried to explain his way out of the misunderstanding, but the damage had been done; he spent considerable time resolving the situation. The moral? Prepare for the meeting and stick to specific job activities instead of drifting into secondary issues.

Evaluating someone in any manner that does not directly reflect specific, objective job performance can get you and your company into trouble. It is the responsibility of every manager to protect the company from any situation even resembling discrimination of any kind. Once the local, state, or federal government, a special-interest group, or the union gets involved, your guilt or innocence no longer matters; you are going to be the cause of the expenditure of considerable amounts of the company's time and money. Avoid this problem by conducting your evaluations in a businesslike fashion.

Handling Behavioral Issues as They Arise

An annual performance evaluation with pay review is the appropriate time and place to consider salary and set or evaluate objectives and action steps. It is *not* the place to deal with performance problems.

Managers expect employees who don't understand a part of their job or how to perform it to ask for direction or training immediately, not wait for a scheduled performance review.

Likewise, a manager should immediately react to poor performance and provide additional instruction as soon as he or she realizes something is wrong. Behavioral problems involving attendance, tardiness, policy violations, attitude toward others or work assignments, team involvement, and participation in productivity improvement efforts should also be handled when they arise. Don't put these problems off until the scheduled performance review unless they occur around the time of that review. Waiting for a review to address an attendance or tardiness issue is, in effect, condoning the behavior.

If your company has policies that call for some form of corrective action when employees have problems with attendance, attitude, or personal behavior, use them. These are the appropriate vehicles for handling these issues as soon as they reach the problem stage. Save the evaluation meeting to measure performance against specific job objectives and set new objectives. The only reason to discuss behavioral problems in a formal evaluation meeting is if an employee fails to reach some objective for reasons that are eventually identified as behavioral.

Don't use company performance evaluation forms to record behavior-based problems. Use progressive discipline forms for attendance or tardiness; write up policy violations such as a suspension for smoking in a nonsmoking area on a blank sheet of paper. The same thing goes for situations in which attitude toward others is being dealt with by the management.

Even though performance evaluation forms that provide space for attitudinal or behavioral aspects seem like convenient places to scribble your remarks, avoid the temptation of using them. A simple checkoff item and a brief entry on the "comments" line isn't enough to tell the complete story. Also, filling out the evaluation form and filing it in an employee's file may lead you to postpone the discussion until the scheduled review. Brushing aside a problem is never the way to solve it. Don't let behavioral problems build to the point where considerable productivity is lost. Don't hope that the problems will correct themselves or that something major will occur that will make them easier to resolve. Worst of all, don't adapt to employees with unproductive traits or behavior. The weaknesses or failures of employees are not simply human nature.

The 80/20 rule comes into play in supervising employees, because you probably spend 80 percent of your time dealing with personnel problems created by 20 percent of your staff. The other 80 percent of the people need only about 20 percent of your time. Many companies develop programs and policies directed at the 20 percent employee group and require managers to spend time administering these programs for the other 80 percent as well. But the best strategy is just the opposite: to operate day-to-day with a simple program directed at those employees who make up the majority, who do not need the detailed and involved performance review evaluation techniques. This can be accomplished by devising a performance evaluation system that provides both managers and employees with one-page job content outlines and clear short-term objectives or action steps that can be frequently reviewed for progress. The problems of the other, smaller group can then be handled through the application of a *critical incidents file.*

A critical incidents file is a collection of quick notations, recorded and filed by the manager, on situations involving behavioral issues. Each time you record an entry, you also talk to the employee about the incident and take appropriate action. Whenever you go back to the file to enter a new incident, you are forced to reread the previous entries, thereby getting a feel for the frequency of that employee's deviations from policy or productive work habits. When the time comes to take drastic action, you will have a detailed paper trail of all applicable incidents supporting termination, suspension, or transfer.

The beauty of this type of system is its simplicity. You don't need training to implement it, and no elaborate forms or programs are needed to deal with a small number of employees at the expense of the majority. It assumes that the vast majority of employees will behave as adults and therefore need only normal levels of direction and corrective action, but provides for those with disruptive or childlike tendencies.

Developing Employee-Driven Evaluations

Most performance evaluation programs and forms are designed by outside firms, consultants, or internal human resource staff professionals. But it can be more effective to assemble a team of management and nonmanagement employees to create a customized performance evaluation strategy and format. This approach offers several advantages over the off-the-shelf, externally designed formats, and also over those programs put together by the company's human resources staff. Some of those advantages are:

1. It can be designed to fit the organization and its technology, workforce, customer base, and management goals.
2. Its contents represent the perspective and opinions of both management and nonmanagement personnel, so that everyone feels "ownership" of the program.
3. The program can be introduced to employees in meetings conducted by members of the team, which also increases participation and builds a sense of ownership.
4. When it's time to change the program, the in-house experts who developed it can consider and make needed changes. The company doesn't have to research and purchase an entirely different program or live with an inappropriate one.
5. The organization develops a solid base of informed employees, because team members who learn the business needs and logic behind a performance evaluation strategy can communicate that knowledge to other employees in their respective departments and functions.

The team should be headed by someone with both knowledge of performance evaluation systems and objectives and experience in facilitating a team. The selection of the members of the team is important. Look for people who are knowledgeable about the organization, have a track record of participating, and have open minds about company objectives. A handful of people is enough for the core team; other people can serve as resources when needed. The project may move slowly at first as team members get used to the idea of designing such a program. But it won't take long before all the team members catch on and draw on their own experiences in evaluation.

After reviewing several different types of evaluation formats, one team of management and nonmanagement personnel decided that a rating scale of 1 to 5 would be appropriate. But when the team shared this concept with people in their respective departments, the reaction was not very positive. Very few employees felt that this type of rating could be objectively applied by any manager in the organization.

As the team discussed the situation, it became clear that a yes or no technique, while never mentioned directly by any of the other employees, might be suitable, considering the objections. A format of yes or no questions was developed and eventually approved and installed. The supervisor's form in Exhibit 7-1 is an example of that format.

The team decided that the logical first question for any evaluation program is whether an employee understands the job he or she has been asked to perform. If the answer is no, there is no need for the supervisor to go any further until that issue is cleared up. It's not possible to evaluate the performance of anyone who does not understand the job. First, you'll have to determine why the person doesn't understand. Is it because of lack of proper training, or has the employee been unable to grasp the training? If so, why wasn't the person retained or dropped from the job?

The team also designed a form to be completed by the employee (Exhibit 7-2) and one that can be submitted to internal customers whose input would be helpful in the evaluation process (Exhibit 7-3). Management and the team agreed that it was important to receive input from the employee concerning the same issues that the supervisor was asked to evaluate. This provided some common ground when the discussion about performance was conducted and ensured that the employee being evaluated had given some thought to the evaluation process. The internal customer input was discretionary and in some cases did not apply; but when used, it provided another area for the supervisor and employee to consider during the discussion.

Peer review is another approach incorporating employee-driven input into the evaluation process. Peer review is appropriate in situations where a group of employees depend upon one another to produce the daily goods or service. If the management is not in the middle of things as they are happening,

Exhibit 7-1. Form for supervisor's evaluation of employee performance.

Performance Evaluation

(Supervisor's Form)

Employee Name: _____

Job Title/Dept.: _____

Supervisor: _____

Evaluation Date: _____

1. Does the employee understand his or her job?   Yes _____   No _____

    Comments: _____

2. Does the employee perform the proper tasks?   Yes _____   No _____

    Comments: _____

3. Does the employee finish tasks on time?   Yes _____   No _____

    Comments: _____

4. Does the employee meet quality standards?   Yes _____   No _____

    Comments: _____

5. Does the employee meet the requirements of other employees who depend on him or her?   Yes _____   No _____

    Comments: _____

6. Does the employee contribute ideas that increase efficiencies in the job/department?   Yes _____   No _____

    Comments: _____

Exhibit 7-1. (Continued)

7. Does the employee practice accurate and timely record keeping?
    Yes _____   No _____

    Comments: _____

8. Is the employee meeting additional objectives set for the job/
    department?   Yes _____   No _____

    Comments: _____

9. Does the employee's overall performance meet your requirements?
    Yes _____   No _____

    Comments: _____

Indicate any critical incidents recorded since last written performance
evaluation:

_____

_____

_____

Action planned: _____

Employee Signature: _____   Date: _____
Employee Comments:

_____

_____

_____

Supervisor Signature: _____   Date: _____

Forwarded to: _____

Exhibit 7-2. Form for employee self-evaluation of performance.

Performance Self-Evaluation

Employee's Name: _____

Job Title/Dept.: _____

Supervisor: _____

Evaluation Date: _____

1. Do you feel that you fully understand your job?   Yes _____   No _____

   Comments: _____

2. Do you feel that you perform the proper tasks?   Yes _____   No _____

   Comments: _____

3. Do you feel that you perform your job in a thorough and accurate manner?   Yes _____   No _____

   Comments: _____

4. Are you able to meet the requirements of those employees who depend on you?   Yes _____   No _____

   Comments: _____

5. Do you contribute ideas that increase the efficiencies in your job or department?   Yes _____   No _____

   Comments: _____

6. Have you accomplished any additional objectives that may have been given you?   Yes _____   No _____

   Comments: _____

Exhibit 7-2. (Continued)

7. Do you feel that your performance has met the overall requirements
of your job?   Yes _____   No _____

   Comments: _____

Indicate any other issues or aspects of your job or job performance that
you would like to discuss or feel are important: _____

_____

_____

Do you want this form included in your Personnel File?
Yes _____   No _____

Employee Signature: _____ Date: _____

but instead depends on the group to manage much of the day-
to-day activities and issue resolution, input from peer performance reviews can be helpful. What it amounts to is a collection
of responses to a structured set of questions that are assembled,
by the group doing the review, into one overall comment about
the employee's performance as a member of that group.

To implement a peer review program, tell employees that
the purpose of the process is to get input from team or group
members regarding an employee on whom that group depends
for critical contributions. Explain that the group will not be
asked to recommend pay and that personnel decisions will still
be management's responsibility. Their role is to take an active
part in the process of information gathering. This is better understood by employees who are part of a group incentive pay
system or profit-sharing program in which the efforts of each
member affect the compensation of the group as a whole.

Often employees are concerned that one person who
doesn't like them could create negative issues that would sully
their record. But they get over that concern when they realize
that a boss can do this to an employee under the traditional

Exhibit 7-3. Form for internal customer's evaluation of employee performance.

Performance Evaluation

(Internal Customer Form)

Please complete this form about the performance of _____.

(Employee's name)

Employee's job title/dept.: _____

Employee's supervisor: _____ Request Date: _____

Name of internal customer performing evaluation: _____

Title and Dept.: _____

1. Does the employee understand his or her job as it relates to servicing your department?   Yes _____   No _____

   Comments: _____

2. Does the employee service your department in a thorough and accurate manner?   Yes _____   No _____

   Comments: _____

3. Does the employee work with your personnel in a cooperative and efficient manner?   Yes _____   No _____

   Comments: _____

4. Does the employee's overall performance meet your department's requirements?   Yes _____   No _____

   Comments: _____

Additional comments: _____

_____

Signature: _____ Date: _____

evaluation system, and that in the peer arrangement, the comments of other members would offset any biased evaluation. If an employee is making a valuable contribution to the group effort, the group is not likely to sabotage that person.

The peer evaluation approach is suitable in some circumstances and not in others. Management has to weigh the value of using knowledge that already exists among employees who work closely together and have keen insights into one another's skills and work practices.

Evaluation: The Manager's Report Card

Performance evaluation of subordinates is a report card that measures how well a manager is managing. Because people seldom do everything right the first time, the amount of surveillance given to their activities has a lot to do with the success or failure of those activities. Therefore, a manager's ability to correct misdirection as early as possible will affect that manager's success.

In education, teachers whose students consistently earn high marks generally spend more time evaluating student progress than teachers whose students make less progress. The same is true of managers.

Managers fail because they have not properly directed their employees or not monitored their efforts thoroughly enough to anticipate and correct the poor direction. Successful managers, on the other hand, either direct properly or so thoroughly evaluate the performance of their employees that they can catch and correct misdirection before it turns into failure. President Lincoln, for example, evaluated and turned over his generals frequently during the Civil War in order to ensure results before the situation could get out of hand. Lincoln's constant evaluation, based on expectations he himself set, disturbed most of his generals, who felt that he was meddling. Human nature hasn't changed much; employees still want to work without anyone peering over their shoulders. But only after a person has shown that he or she does not require detailed supervision should that person expect some autonomy in the job.

In order to grade managers on their skill at evaluating employee performance, an organization has to have the correct type of performance evaluation strategy or program in place. Evaluation programs that rate soft aspects of employee input, such as their ability to work with others, work ethic, company loyalty, or effort put forth, are simply too easy to tilt in any direction a manager feels is comfortable or convenient. They make it easy for a manager to avoid conflict with an employee whose performance is less than desired, process a pay increase that may not really be deserved but will make the manager's job easier, or do just enough evaluation to comply with company policy.

But a strategy or program that requires objectives or action steps with deadlines as part of the direction and evaluation of each employee can more easily measure or indicate a manager's skill and practice. Managers quickly learn that even if they can't measure well, they can measure often. Managers are more likely to say, "Don't tell me you've been busy; tell me what you've gotten done," if they know that the evaluation is going to be reviewed by someone else for relevance and objectivity.

Relevant, objective employee performance evaluations offer several benefits to an organization. They indicate how skilled management is at monitoring progress toward goals. When staff needs are increasing or decreasing, evaluations help a company make decisions about whom to promote or where to reduce the workforce. They let an organization go back and construct a history of an employee's performance and management's reactions to that performance—essential in making or defending a decision to separate an employee from the company. Especially if a situation leads to litigation, accurate, clear documents are vital, because they are often interpreted by people who have little or no knowledge of the individuals involved. A manager's knowledge of the purpose and role of performance evaluations in these situations and his or her ability to conduct and record those meetings may determine how much a company spends to react to these human resources issues.

Therefore, it makes sense to evaluate how well managers evaluate. Good managers deserve to have their efforts acknowledged, and managers who are not producing at the level expected need intervention and assistance in order to do a better job of evaluating and get better results.

CHAPTER 8

The Evaluation Meeting

There are two types of performance evaluation: formal, scheduled evaluations that result in sit-down sessions between manager and subordinate, and informal, day-to-day evaluations in which manager and subordinate exchange impromptu comments about performance issues. The informal performance review is vital because it ensures the daily output that sustains the company. This direction and evaluation is almost second nature and provides the pressure that we commonly refer to as "work." The formal, scheduled review has structure to it, and that structure, in its various versions, is the subject of this chapter.

Why Managers Hate Evaluation

For many managers, evaluation is an uncomfortable process even when the news is good. Tell people that they've done a good job, and they may expect a raise you can't afford or a promotion that isn't available. Tell them that they've done a good or average job, and they'll be disappointed. No one wants to hear that he or she is average. Tell folks that they've done a poor job, and you have angry employees or a potential confrontation.

An employee who enters your office for a performance evaluation meeting is almost trick-or-treating. If he or she doesn't get a treat, you can expect some form of trick later. Because managers don't like tricks, many simply give out treats. Others actually trick their employees by surprising them during the meeting—a major violation of the evaluation process, which, when performed well, contains no surprises on either side. These managers never give a review that makes the employee feel good. The author of the following anonymous "poem" obviously felt tricked; that's why he slipped these lines into the in-box of a manager who had just completed a review:

I Received My Performance Review Today, and Am I Mad!

My supervisor conducted today, as it is his duty,
My annual performance review, and it was a beauty.
He said that the money, while it wasn't much,
Shouldn't cause me to protest, or to fuss.
My performance, he continued, was really adequate,
Although there was an aspect that I apparently neglect.
Performance, he explained, was no longer a measure.
Instead, he went on, commitment was the lever.
Commitment was defined to mean hours and pace.
That is, how long and fast you run around this place.
Others, it appears, have more of this knack.
Therefore, they will get the purse; I will get the strap.
My mission, he went on to say, was to fill the hours of the day.
And to try, because he's busy, to stay out of the way.
I've thought about the message, contained in all this wisdom.
And have reduced it down to nugget-size, for easier transmission.
It seems that he has struck a blow to kill an age-old trait.
That is, working smarter, not harder, is now just excess freight.

Tricks like this have no business in the evaluation meeting. No one should go into a performance evaluation meeting and produce information that will come as a complete surprise to the other person. A boss who does this has been withholding important performance requirements or results until the review date. Perhaps performance was not managed on a daily basis. Or it was evaluated daily, but nothing was done or said about it until the annual review. Neither possibility makes sense from a business management standpoint. A performance review meeting should never result in an ambush for either side.

Another reason why both managers and employees dread the evaluation meeting or interview is that it involves one person passing judgment on the other and makes both people uncomfortable. The managers doing the evaluations and conducting the meetings feel almost embarrassed to play a role they do not feel confident they are equipped to play. They are called upon to make evaluation judgments using insufficient information—information that may not back up a firm position on whether an employee's performance is bad, good, average, or barely acceptable. When the supporting information is vague and subjective, both parties may feel that the meeting is a waste of time or that the results are inappropriate or inadequate. Either way, the process loses credibility.

Because managers feel that they will be unable to support or defend their positions should an employee seriously challenge or question their judgments, evaluation meetings end up being very short—too brief to provide much in terms of positive results. And there *should* be positive results, because performance evaluation meetings have one major goal: to determine the future status within the organization of the individuals being evaluated. Yes, meetings evaluate past performance and accommodate or reward individuals for what they've already done— but only in order to anticipate the future. If an employee hasn't done a good job since his or her last review and pay increase, the company doesn't get its money back. All the company can do is make sure that it gets a better return on its future investment in the employee.

If the goal of the evaluation process is to determine the future status of the employee within the organization, then it is critical that both employee and manager have confidence in the evaluation process, including the dreaded meeting. This chapter introduces four steps that will increase the credibility of the evaluation meeting and create more confidence in the outcome. The specific improvement steps are:

1. Collecting better input data
2. Creating greater confidence in the process
3. Conducting more-productive meetings
4. Improving personnel utilization in the future

Let's look at these steps one at a time.

Collecting Better Input Data

Input data is the information you bring to the meeting to back up your perception of someone's performance. When you and the employee both have valid performance information to examine during the meeting, you can discuss substantive issues instead of subjective, how-I-think-you're-doing perceptions. Good input data help both of you back up your assertions, so that you can feel confident that the meeting can accurately evaluate past performance and determine suitable future assignments.

Briefly, the input data you need to prepare consist of:

- Critical incidents file
- Objectives and action steps
- Performance evaluation forms
- Job descriptions
- Compensation changes

When you take direction seriously, this evidence will be easy to gather, because you will have been carefully monitoring how each employee is performing against agreed-upon goals and objectives. But simply bringing this information to the meeting is not enough. The key to effective employee performance evaluation meetings is preparation. That means organizing and reviewing materials ahead of time, drafting a list or script of items to cover, and planning how to present those items to the employee.

When you schedule the meeting, give the employee a copy of the employee self-evaluation form shown in Exhibit 7-2 of Chapter 7. Let the employee know that he or she is expected to complete this form and come to the meeting prepared to discuss it. Meanwhile, you need to sit down and review the input data materials so that you are prepared to discuss them. Remember, your goal is to have *no* surprises. An effective evaluation meeting confirms two people's mutual perceptions. While you will need to discuss any points of disagreement, those points shouldn't be news to either one of you.

The more time you spend preparing and organizing your input data, the more productive the evaluation meeting will be.

If you're not prepared for the meeting, you'll get stuck in a morass of small talk, or the two of you will disagree over issues that aren't critical or that you can't back up with facts. And for the process to be respected by everyone in your company, you need to fully participate in gathering, organizing, and preparing information for the meeting. Remember, you're evaluating half of the employee's waking hours. Take your responsibility seriously, and prepare.

Critical Incidents File

The critical incidents file, discussed in Chapter 7, is used to document usually negative incidents such as an unexplained absence or a policy violation. (The critical incidents file can also be used to record positive performance occurrences.) Review these negative incidents before the meeting in order to discuss them once again. Even if you and the employee have already discussed them, it's important to provide reinforcement. Ignoring such incidents during a performance review could imply that they were not all that critical after all.

Objectives and Action Steps

Objectives and action steps are at the heart of the evaluation process and will take up a good portion of the interview. You have probably discussed the overall status of an employee's responsibilities in previous review sessions conducted during the year. But in order to review the employee's yearly performance contribution, you need to devote meeting time to the record of the employee's efforts.

The status of the employee's performance on any objectives or action steps can be divided into three categories:

1. Objectives or action steps clearly achieved
2. Objectives or action steps clearly not achieved
3. Objectives or action steps with uncertain results

Categories 1 and 2 can be handled in a straightforward manner. Items in category 3, however, need to be reviewed to determine the cause or causes of the uncertain results. Did the employee fail to perform? Did someone else's failure to perform affect this person's performance? Were objectives not achieved because of circumstances beyond the company's control? Sometimes the real problem rests in the design of the objective or action step. The objective or action step may have been impossible to accomplish from its inception. Whatever the cause, missed objectives or action steps need to be thoroughly evaluated and discussed in order to determine the future status of the employee with the company, function, or department.

Performance Evaluation Forms

Make sure to distribute and gather any forms used in your performance appraisal program. If the employee is to complete forms, make sure he or she gets them well in advance of the meeting. Be sure to conduct and gather any other performance evaluation comments your company may require, such as peer reviews, team reviews, or performance reports from internal or outside customers. The format of these forms doesn't really matter, so long as they allow everyone to provide thoughts and impressions.

Job Descriptions

Review the employee's current job description before the meeting and revise it to include any recent changes in what the employee is expected to do. If you plan to change or expand the employee's responsibilities, prepare a draft of the job description that describes the new responsibilities. Your meeting agenda should include time to discuss the job description so that you can communicate any new job content elements to the employee and record the fact that the discussion took place.

Compensation Changes

Some managers don't discuss compensation changes during the performance evaluation meeting because they think employees will be too distracted by the money to concentrate on the other issues being discussed. Others wait in order to allow insights that come out of the meeting to be factored into the pay decision.

What this really says is that the manager expects to be surprised at the meeting by something that the employee knew but the manager didn't. Remember, if you've done a thorough job of directing and evaluating all along, this shouldn't happen.

In my view, the only performance evaluation meeting in which compensation can be avoided is one that results in the employee's termination. In every other case, the employee will be thinking about what the evaluation means for her or his pay-check. Even if you postpone compensation to a follow-up meeting, employees will still try to figure out what size or percentage pay increase they deserve or will get.

People work for money. They want to know that their pay is fair. That's why you should begin evaluation sessions with a clear idea of what the proper pay increase for that employee should be, if the schedule calls for a pay review at that time. If the employee disagrees with the amount, you can discuss it, but the discussion has to start from some figure, and that initial number has to come from you, not the employee.

Employee Preparation

To ensure a productive meeting, the employee also needs to prepare. Many people walk into their performance evaluation session without any idea of what is expected of them, and assume that they should be passive listeners. Some perk up only when a pay increase is mentioned. But if the meeting is to improve the utilization of the employee, both parties must take an active role.

The employee needs to completely understand what has been measured, how it has been measured, how her or his performance stacks up against previous expectations, and what the future expectations are for him or her. For this to happen, the employee has to be interested and involved. One way to create that interest and involvement is to ask the employee to complete the self-evaluation form shown in Exhibit 7-2 (Chapter 7). Another is to provide an instruction sheet that tells employees what their role is and how they are expected to act during their performance evaluation session. Employees can gain considerably from suggestions like those in the handout shown in Exhibit 8-1.

Exhibit 8-1. Instruction sheet to prepare employees for their role in a performance evaluation meeting.

Ensuring a Productive Performance Evaluation Meeting

The responsibility for making your scheduled evaluation meeting a productive one is not only your supervisor's but yours as well. Like your supervisor, you must understand your role in the meeting and your responsibilities in preparing for it. The following suggestions will help you to make the evaluation meeting as productive as possible.

1. Thoroughly complete any material requested of you so that your input can be incorporated into the meeting.
2. Anticipate and write out any issues or questions that you might want to address at the meeting.
3. During the meeting, be open and attentive to issues you and your supervisor discuss.
4. Work with your supervisor at gaining insight into past performance, as well as future assignments and tasks.
5. Ask relevant questions and expect straightforward answers or responses.
6. Be businesslike, involved, and growth-oriented during the meeting, and expect the same from your supervisor.

Input for Management Employees

If you are evaluating a manager or a supervisor, you will need to gather information about the person's management skills. If your organization does not have a structured, detailed form, list aspects of the manager's responsibilities to discuss during the meeting on a blank sheet of paper. The following list represents the variety of skills to consider when appraising people who manage or supervise functions or other employees:

Skill	*Operating Results*
Planning	_____
Organizing	_____
Coordinating	_____

Skill	*Operating Results*
Delegating	_____
Controlling	_____
Supervising	_____

Don't merely evaluate traits. Look at the effect each element has on operating results. Planning, for example, that involves use of a planner book and a schedule that is followed no matter what else occurs may not be a virtue; it may, in fact, be a real detriment to effectively managing a fast-paced, highly changeable function.

It is not easy to measure or evaluate such skills as coordinating or delegating. Instead of focusing on whether or not the manager practices the skill, examine the impact the application of the skill has on the overall performance results of that manager's total job.

Weighting the various aspects may help. For example, an operation that is chaotic by nature may need less emphasis on organizing day-to-day activity and more on supervising that activity. Think through these issues before the meeting so that you can explore them there; opportunities to do so don't come up every day.

Avoiding Confrontation

Every well-prepared manager and every interested employee hopes for a performance evaluation meeting free of major disagreements or disputes. Fortunately, most performance evaluation meetings are trouble-free—but there are times when things can become uncomfortable, even confrontational. The best approach a manager can take is to consider this possibility, anticipate any areas that might develop into a confrontation, and prepare a response or reaction.

Don't prepare to take a hard line on these issues. Stay open and understanding. Simply identify potential issues ahead of time, and anticipate and gather any additional input that will help you deal with them and maintain a professional demeanor.

How the issues are eventually handled depends on what comes out of the discussion.

Differences of opinion are part and parcel of measuring performance. While they cannot be ignored, they should not be feared. If you and your subordinate are properly prepared with real data and information, both of you can handle these issues with a maximum amount of objectivity and a minimum amount of emotion.

Creating Greater Confidence in the Process

The first step in creating confidence in any process is to apply that process consistently. This is especially true for a process as potentially volatile as performance evaluation meetings.

Confidence can be described as reliance, assurance, or trust. Each of these words indicates a need for consistency. Only when all employees know that the process of measuring and evaluating performance is applied to everyone in the same manner and that the process itself is timely, accurate, and fair can there be confidence. Employees know that they will have different bosses during their tenure at a company. They want records of their good performance to be in the files and available to the next boss. They don't want to have to prove themselves all over again with each and every new supervisor. Only a consistent and documented performance management process can provide this.

Another important ingredient in building confidence is understanding. When people understand that evaluation helps justify actions the organization takes on behalf of its employees, they will want to see the process implemented consistently. They need to know that there are thoughtful, accurate records that justify retention and promotion as well as termination. Besides helping a company make and defend decisions about utilizing employees, a consistently implemented evaluation program protects employees from impulsive or vindictive acts and decisions. When employees understand this, they will be more than willing to do their part to make the program run smoothly.

The only way to ensure consistency is to set down some guidelines or rules for the game. Performance evaluation is no different from any other activity. Left to their own devices, some managers do a thorough job, others do only the minimum, and still others will not bother to hold evaluation meetings at all. That's why it's critical to develop and circulate a company policy about the purpose, procedure, and application of the performance evaluation process. Managers need a document that spells out what is expected of them in dealing with this vital responsibility. It needn't include every little step, but it should outline the framework and the schedule. Without such a policy, a company's top management is saying that when it comes to evaluation—in fact, when it comes to plain old performance—anything goes.

A performance evaluation program or policy can be as simple as Exhibit 8-2.

If employees at all levels are to have confidence in the performance evaluation process, they must know that there is a procedure that managers must follow. If they are to trust the process, they must see the procedure enforced by the company. And to be enforced, a policy must be clearly expressed, which is why the general purpose and procedure must be committed to paper.

Once this policy is posted, it's essential that reviews be held when promised. Nothing does more to cause scheduled evaluation meetings to start off wrong than not holding them at the time they are scheduled. If an annual review is postponed, and fourteen or fifteen months pass before the review is held, an employee may rightly see this as management's disregard of "promises made."

Managers must conduct the reviews and meetings within a reasonable time. Being out of town, vacations, or a heavy workload may seem like valid excuses for delaying a meeting, but they are still excuses. A manager's ability to meet these commitments should be a part of his or her performance evaluation. To make sure managers review employees in a timely manner, many companies refuse to process retroactive or recommended pay increases that are not supported by a performance review. No manager wants employee pay increases to be delayed because of his or her failure to react on time. Companies that do

Exhibit 8-2. Simple performance evaluation program.

Purpose

This Performance Evaluation Program has been developed by management for the following purposes:

1. To evaluate and communicate individual performance
2. To address performance issues through corrective action and/or job content change
3. To establish and communicate job and performance expectations
4. To provide documentation in a valid format

Procedure

Step 1: A monthly list indicating those individuals scheduled for annual evaluation and meeting during the month will be distributed to managers and posted.

Step 2: The respective manager will, within one week of the scheduled evaluation date:

a. Perform the evaluation using required company forms.
b. Instruct the employee about his or her input into the process.
c. Conduct the communication meeting with the individual.
d. Follow up on any issues such as corrective action, job content change, or pay adjustment.
e. Document the results of the evaluation and record them in the individual's personnel file.

allow the practice of retroactive or unsupported pay increases are simply condoning poor management practices.

Conducting More-Productive Meetings

Once you have assembled input that outlines an employee's past performance and future expectations, you need to organize it. The following sequence can guide you through the evaluation session. Keep it on your desk and, as you move through the process or meeting, check off items as they are completed. This allows you to know at any point during the discussion just what has been covered and what remains to be covered. It provides focus and ensures that all of the required actions are included in the process.

Manager's Evaluation Meeting Guide

1. State the purpose of the meeting.
2. Review the employee's self-evaluation.
3. Review the manager's employee evaluation.
4. Discuss any differences and reach understanding.
5. Outline future performance and job expectations.
6. Discuss any appropriate pay adjustments.
7. Schedule any follow-up sessions or next evaluation date.

Use this guide to develop an agenda and you can be confident that you are addressing the correct items. Using it and sticking to it will also make your evaluation meetings more productive, so that you can finish in thirty to sixty minutes.

The following techniques will help you develop a demeanor or style that facilitates a productive meeting:

❑ *Invite open discussion.* Start the meeting by making it clear that it's fine for the employee to express disagreement. State that disagreements should be kept as objective and specific as possible. Acknowledge that although keeping emotion out is almost impossible, disagreements should not be ignored simply because they may be uncomfortable or difficult. If the individual received a description of his or her role in the meeting (refer back to Exhibit 8-1), your comments will underscore a point already made. If not, you'll have to make this ground rule clear.

❑ *Keep to specifics.* Refer to the critical incidents file material or any other record of performance issues. Avoid drifting into subjective areas of personality or traits. Comments like "You seem to be the kind of person who . . ." will make the employee feel that you are generalizing or stereotyping. Remember, you're not evaluating the person's self-image or designing jobs around his or her personality. You are paying the person to do a job or achieve objectives that the organization needs to have accomplished in order to meet its goals. Providing every individual with a job that fits his or her immediate needs is not one of those goals.

❑ *Avoid employee comparisons.* Allowing the discussion to include references to or comparisons with other employees is seldom productive and only makes it harder to evaluate the employee's performance. It deflects the spotlight away from the issue, which is how this person performed relative to job expectations and what future expectations will be. People being evaluated often want to tell why their ability to perform was affected by how others performed. People *do* affect one another—but as a manager, it's your responsibility to continually manage these relationships and not let them surface for the first time during an annual evaluation meeting. These issues should be brought up in departmental or team meetings as a part of the daily management effort.

Also, what goes around comes around. If you allow someone to discuss others or permit inappropriate comments, the person being evaluated at the meeting will assume that he or she is being talked about in meetings with others. Your ability to guard confidential or sensitive information becomes suspect.

❑ *Highlight significance.* Which is more effective: telling an employee that his or her performance was above or below expectations, or noting that because his or her performance was above or below expectations, the company is either more successful or closing down? Understanding the significance of one's actions can considerably influence how an individual acts in the future. Managers need to be able to explain why certain actions are important and what they mean to the company or department as a whole. Paying attention to the significance of an employee's successes or failures ensures that the employee knows that the manager is not making something out of nothing. It prevents people from feeling picked on, set up for failure, or discriminated against. It also keeps people better informed about the overall influence of their role in the organization.

❑ *Be decisive.* Don't put up with excessive disagreement if you feel you've done a good job of measuring and evaluating

---

Three Rules for Productive Evaluation Meetings

1. Don't say anything more if there is nothing more to say.
2. Don't say it here if it should have been said somewhere else.
3. If there wasn't anywhere else to say it, say it here. Don't leave it unsaid.

---

performance. Discussions can often become a battle of wills. Be firm and decisive when you get to a point where you feel that all the information is in and it is time to move on. If the performance is not there, and others under you do seem to be able to perform, you have to face the possibility that the individual you are dealing with is just not up to the job. Make sure that the person understands the standards he or she is expected to meet, and hold him or her to those standards. When you are one-on-one and face-to-face with a person is the appropriate and best time to confront that person with all the issues.

Improving Personnel Utilization in the Future

The goal of effective employee evaluation meetings is to determine and communicate what the employee can do from that point on to increase his or her value to the organization and receive a fair reward for that increased value. Of course, not all of this takes place during the meeting. As a manager, you have developed some direction or status for the employee prior to the meeting. Now, you need to match what the employee has to offer with the human resources needs your organization will have in the near future.

To create a real plan for the future of the employee, you need that employee's input, which you collect before and discuss during the meeting. You should have a tentative proposal regarding the individual's future status when the meeting starts—a proposal that includes changes in responsibilities or salary. As the meeting progresses and you gather input from the employee, you should hear things that support the proposed future status. At an appropriate moment in the meeting, you can present those changes, or lack of changes, and discuss them with the employee.

Your goal is to improve not just an employee's job performance, but the performance of all the personnel in your department or division. There's a difference between an employee who performs at 100 percent in a job whose design limits the way he or she utilizes skills that are valuable to the organization or department, and that same employee performing at 100 percent in an expanded set of job responsibilities.

In both cases the person's performance is 100 percent or meets expectations. However, in the expanded job, that employee is being much better utilized by the organization. Assuming that the employee gets more money for those additional responsibilities, both the employee and the company benefit. This is the goal of the evaluation meeting: to look back at what the employee has really done and to plan, from that information, what the employee can do next that will be of even greater value.

Assuming everything goes as expected, new objectives, goals, action steps, or job content is outlined and documented for future evaluation. This structured, additional step makes the meeting more than just a review of past performance; it is the start of improved utilization of the employee in the days to come.

"You've done well; keep up the good work" is not enough. "You've done well, and here's what we expect from you in the future" is what the meeting should produce.

CHAPTER 9

Using Evaluations

Managers are paid to determine, initiate, oversee, and evaluate action or activities. To evaluate, they must continually reassess their human resources and redirect, replace, or retrain all or some of them to ensure meeting the unit's objectives. Evaluation, in itself, is only part of that responsibility. Once an employee's past performance has been accurately evaluated, the manager needs to determine that person's future role in the organization, based on exhibited skills and their application. This chapter looks at how to use the information gathered during the evaluation itself and the subsequent meeting or meetings conducted with the employee. To merely file evaluations away after discussing them with employees is to disregard the purpose of the evaluation process: to continually improve the utilization of the organization's human resources in accomplishing the organization's objectives.

How Evaluations Should Be Used

Performance evaluations are used for a number of purposes. The business entities that use evaluations and the purposes for which they use them are as follows:

Company

1. To support pay changes
2. To maintain a record of employee performance

Manager

1. To monitor employee performance
2. To communicate employee performance
3. To determine employees' coaching and training needs
4. To plan future departmental employee needs
5. To justify pay changes
6. To maintain a record of employee performance

Employee

1. To understand performance status from the company perspective
2. To relate "fairness" of pay to performance and responsibilities
3. To plan a career within or outside the company

Both the company and the employee use evaluation information in a passive manner. It's the manager who has the greatest opportunity or responsibility for directly using that information. The six purposes listed are unique to the manager, and make up a major portion of what managers are hired and paid to do.

Items one and two contribute valuable information to an employee evaluation. Items three, four, five, and six *should* directly result from the evaluation process. However, they are the very activities that many managers tend to push aside for attention at a later date—even though they are also the very activities that can transform a somewhat effective organization into an organization that is as effective as it can be.

How Evaluations Should *Not* Be Used

Missing from the list of uses for performance evaluations is a common application that is actually a misapplication: using performance evaluations to design jobs around individuals. Evaluations should never be used in this way. Throughout this book, I've stressed that jobs should never be designed to accommodate someone simply because that person cannot do what the company needs done. The same is true for people who have skills or talents that the company doesn't need. Just because a person can do something doesn't mean that he or she should do it. No matter what a person's level of skill or performance, jobs should be designed only around what needs to be done within the organization. Accommodating employees is not appropriate for any organization that has to be efficient in order to survive.

Family-owned businesses often create jobs to support members of the family. At first glance, these jobs appear to be important to the business, but a closer look reveals that they wouldn't be missed if they were eliminated. Managers sometimes redesign a job to accommodate a poorly performing employee by reassigning elements the person has trouble performing to someone else while the poor performer does a part-time job at full-time wages. A variation on this theme is adding unnecessary elements to a job in order to justify a promotional pay increase for an above-average performer who wants a promotion but has no legitimate way to move up.

Some argue that this approach is a good investment because it keeps a good employee until a solid promotion opens up. After all, that's cheaper than losing and replacing the person, isn't it? Not really. When that real promotion appears, the company will have to give another pay increase on top of the false one. That misspent money is there for as long as that employee is in the organization. It can also create pressure to increase other employees' wages to maintain internal pay equity.

Empire building is another dangerous outcome of false promotions. Some managers inflate or create jobs in order to obligate others and build their own power. These managers are emphasizing their own needs, not the needs of the organization. The problem only gets worse when these managers are themselves promoted. When they get more power, they create even more artificial promotions. It's hard for a higher-level manager to believe that this person's request for another hire or additional pay dollars is genuine.

Don't play fast and loose by giving promotions that simply aren't real. It is better to inform the employee that the above-average performance has been noted and that as soon as a promotion opens up, the person's record will certainly be considered.

Designing jobs to accommodate individuals is *not* the same as redesigning equipment and procedures to make jobs available to individuals with handicaps or those whose situations do not allow them to operate as most others do. In these situations, the job responsibilities, content, and objectives remain the same and performance is generally evaluated in the same manner. The procedures and processes, however, may have been adjusted or altered.

Performance Categories and How to Handle Them

Many performance evaluation programs are overloaded with categories. Some ask managers to divide employees into as many as eight or nine performance categories—a level of subtlety that not only isn't needed, but also causes the process to become entirely too subjective. In my view, a performance evaluation program needs only three categories of performance. An employee's performance either:

1. *Exceeds* expectations or requirements
2. *Meets* expectations or requirements.
3. *Falls below* expectations or requirements

In this case, expectations or requirements are the level of performance that a company has the right to "demand" from the person holding the job and taking the paycheck. It's like cashing a check. When you submit a check, you make an on-demand payment request. You have a right to that payment as long as you can prove your identity. The level of performance defined as "expectations or requirements" is similar. Employees should accept that what you are demanding, expecting, or requiring is fair and comparable to what other companies demand in similar jobs.

While some might think that the distribution of people throughout this performance range in an organization would follow a bell-shaped curve—that is, approximately 20 percent at the "exceeds" level, 60 percent at the "meets" level, and 20 percent at the "below" level—that isn't true of an organization at any specific time. When signs indicate that an employee is performing below expectations, most managers deal with the problem by transferring the employee to another job, retraining him or her for the original job, or terminating the employee. In too many cases, the standards may be lowered or the job content changed to accommodate the problem performer. As a result, most managers will claim that they do not have anyone who is performing below expectations.

In reality, some people, promotions, and reassignments just don't work out. There has to be a procedure to identify them and a performance classification that covers the lowest level of performance.

Within each of the three major categories are subcategories, which are defined below.

Employees Who Exceed Expectations or Requirements

- *Immediate promotion potential.* These individuals consistently perform their jobs at such high levels of quality and quantity that a promotion seems to be past due. They also accomplish specific objectives established for the job from the overall business plan. These individuals may be working at a job that is beneath their basic set of skills and general capabilities, perhaps because no promotional openings have been available. Without question, they could perform the responsibilities of a higher position.
- *Eventual promotion potential.* The performance of employees in this subcategory has been progressing at a rate that is normal for the job and typical for an incumbent who is expected to progress to the next higher-level job within a year or two. Their performance includes normal duties as well as objectives assigned based on the overall business plan.

Employees Who Meet Expectations or Requirements

- *Immediate promotion potential*
- *Eventual promotion potential*

❑ *Questionable promotion potential.* These are employees who barely manage to perform normal duties and should not be considered ready for promotion until they increase their skill base, develop a higher degree of motivation, and sustain a higher level of performance for a significant period of time.

Employees Who Fall Below Expectations or Requirements

❑ *Possible retention.* Employees in this subcategory are not performing up to the expectations of the job and may not be accomplishing objectives that were assigned in addition to the regular duties.
❑ *Not retainable.* These are employees who are not performing and from whom there is little hope of getting what you need in terms of performance. These are bad hires, bad promotions, and bad transfers. Often, these people have received a rating of "possible retention" in their previous evaluation.

Evaluation makes reality clear: Employees are either exceeding, meeting, or performing below expectations. However, not all managers are willing or able to face hard issues. Thus, it is in translating reality into the proper actions and communicating them to employees that some managers fail.

But in order to improve the utilization of people and maximize the return on your investment in payroll dollars, you need to develop the right kind of response to each type of performance. The end result or objective of any performance evaluation strategy is to improve the effectiveness of the organization. Measuring performance and then failing to use that information to influence the future performance levels is not managing. It is simply gathering useless data.

Handling Employees Who Deserve Immediate or Eventual Promotion

The immediate or eventual availability of a promotion for the employee concerned is, of course, the determining factor in how people with these ratings are handled. If the manager can tell the person that there are plans to promote him or her, that is the direction the evaluation meeting should take. Discuss performance history and evaluated level of performance first, then give the employee's rating and the reward for that performance— perhaps promotion to a certain job, at a certain rate of pay, effective on a specific date. The reward for an individual considered "eventual promotion potential" may include the possibility of a promotion within a specific time frame.

When there is no opportunity for a promotion in the foreseeable future, should you discuss this with the employee, or simply say that he or she is doing a good job? If your company has communicated openly with all employees and been candid about their ratings and the implications of these ratings, the employee will want to know his or her promotion potential, when to expect a promotion, and whether other employees are ahead of him or her for those opportunities. These are difficult questions, but an employee has the right to know the answers.

The only way to deal with this situation is to make it clear that the future is unknown. Don't avoid questions because they are difficult. When you can't answer a question, simply say, "I can't answer that at this time." Any other approach jeopardizes your credibility and the credibility of the performance evaluation process.

Avoid creating any unreasonable expectations. They almost always lead to disappointment, which interferes with productivity and ends up creating another time-consuming problem for the manager and the organization to solve. Many managers make unnecessary promises because they fear that high-achieving employees will slack off without prospects of a promotion. But that simply isn't true. People who do a good job will generally continue to perform unless the company completely ignores their contributions. Instead of making a false or vague promise, tell them that they are doing an outstanding job and that they will be among the first to be considered for the next available promotion.

Another factor in determining whether a person is promotable is the position he or she is being considered for. Lean or flat organizations require quite a bit of stretch when an individual moves up in responsibility. The person may be taking over duties that include unfamiliar elements, or be transferred into entirely different functions in order to gain experience in that discipline. A smaller percentage of people will be eligible for promotion in these organizations than in a more pyramid-shaped one. Transfers can sometimes be called promotions and include pay increases because the company is really recognizing that the "promoted" individual is capable of learning new skills quickly.

Where a company falls in this regard determines the guidelines for promotion potential in the performance evaluation ratings. This, in turn, requires clear communication by the evaluating manager when discussing the evaluations with the employee. Management and nonmanagement personnel need to understand the distinction between a promotion and a transfer.

Handling Promotions to Management-Level Positions

When an employee is to be promoted into a management-level position, you can devote the performance evaluation meeting to discussing aspects of the new job. Doing so gives the employee feedback about future performance expectations and lets you prepare him or her for increased responsibilities when they eventually occur. This gives substance to the meeting and may take the edge off the open-ended issue of when a promotion will be available.

Some of the aspects of management-level work may seem like personality traits that people either possess or lack. But the first step in preparing someone for a management-level position or a position with greater management responsibilities is to make the individual aware of the traits and practices she or he needs in order to achieve the measurable results expected from her or him as a manager. Here are a few of the traits or tools that managers need to "own" in order to be successful:

> ❑ Managers must be action-oriented rather than reaction-oriented. They must be goal setters who don't let the events around them determine what they do over short or long periods of time.

❑ Managers need a sense of completion. They need to be able to see things through to the end, often making adjustments along the way. Loose ends are not acceptable to good managers.

❑ Managers must have a sense of what is important. Whether they set objectives for themselves or for others, they must know how to prioritize on the basis of the organization's needs and goals.

❑ Managers need to understand the limits of control that they have, or should have, over events or other people.

❑ Managers need to think in terms of costs and results—two key factors that should be used to measure all actions.

❑ Managers need to have and develop a sense of ownership regarding problems and the organization. Individuals who have a feeling of detachment toward problems and the company cannot be effective managers.

❑ Managers need mental toughness when it comes to handling disappointments, adversity, and resistance. They can't waste time lamenting what might have been or complaining about situations. Not only is that unproductive; it causes problems to become bigger than they would have been had they simply been dealt with right away.

❑ Managers need to become comfortable with being uncomfortable. There are too many options and issues in management for people to expect to always feel comfortable with their responsibilities. Managers have to deal with this reality.

❑ Managers need to avoid being intimidated by people or events—this is essential if a person wants to manage from an objective perspective.

❑ Managers should avoid becoming committed to processes rather than service or effectiveness. Processes have to be continually reviewed and changed in order to make progress in levels of service and effectiveness.

❑ Managers must understand that an individual's work ethic or personality can't always be changed. Often, the only way to change the culture of a business environment is to change the types of people working there. Facing up to these kinds of issues is what performance evaluation and human resources management are all about. It does no good to send your ducks to eagle school.

Managers have to have farmerlike skills: They have to be able to handle any situation that comes up, and they often have to work to schedules that are not under their control. When it's time to plant, the farmer can't look to the sky and ask for a few extra days because the seed is not available yet. When it's time to harvest, there can be no excuses about equipment not being ready. Successful farm managers work around problems like the weather, and they make sure that their employees know what has to be done and by when. Farmers know that there can be no adjustments to the overall schedules and that excuses are worthless. A sense of urgency is required in these jobs.

Handling Employees With Questionable Promotion Potential

People who work very hard to just meet their job expectations and can't seriously be considered promotable need coaching and evaluation from their manager. If the employee begins to produce results with a normal amount of effort, promotion might be a possibility. But the odds are that the employee knows that he or she is running hard to just stay in one place and that a promotion would be a prelude to failure. The theme of these evaluation meetings is, "What can we do to make the desired results come easier to you?" If the proper training and direction has been and is being given, you can assume that the employee has advanced as far as possible in that job classification or profession.

The other possibility is the person has the potential to do more but produces just enough to avoid a bad review. For some reason the employee does not want to make any additional effort, even though he or she has the skills. In such situations, some managers like to become motivators. They think that by giving a larger than usual pay raise or, in extreme cases, a gift promotion, an employee who is performing at a borderline or fringe level will be awakened and motivated. It seldom works, and when it does, the improvement is short-lived.

This type of borderline performer may feel that the manager is an easy mark and begin testing the manager's judgment and gullibility. In this Bear and the Jelly Beans approach to handling fringe performers, the manager tries to keep the bear happy and at bay by continually giving it jelly beans. But when the jelly beans are gone, the manager has a problem bear, and hands that smell of jelly beans.

The best way to work with employees whose performance is adequate but who have the potential to improve is to closely analyze their performance. Many times an employee's overall performance is hindered by lack of skill in one or two job elements. Above-average performers are seldom better than the average person in all aspects of their job; they simply do one or two parts of it better than others and are average in the rest. Like character actors in the movies, they are not stars, but they are better than bit players. The character actor has a characteristic that allows him or her to earn an above-average living in that business. Only close study will reveal the nature of that characteristic among actors and nonactors alike.

By shortening the review cycles and isolating the elements of the job, you can often discern which element or elements the person is having trouble performing. Comparisons to the performance of other employees can identify where the troubled individual is behind the curve. This technique is standard in sales. When a salesperson is having trouble producing the numbers expected, the manager will often go out on calls with that person and try to determine which aspects need attention. Once these are identified, the rest is usually easy. Apply this approach in any situation where the reason for less than anticipated performance is unclear.

The most efficient way to analyze performance is to ask the employee to log her or his daily tasks and the amount of time spent on each element. Reviewing this log at the end of each day or week and asking how easy or hard the person found each task will quickly identify areas needing attention.

Although it takes only a week or two to discover the problem element, correcting it is not as easy. However, with journal in hand, you and the employee can talk in specific terms instead of tossing around generalities. Sometimes the problem is as simple as one little piece of the job that the person has not understood or has not been thoroughly trained in. Giving your attention to these types of details provides greater value from the company's payroll dollars and justifies management jobs.

This is another form of measurement—a key element in management's list of responsibilities. If you can improve department or company efficiency by just 5 percent through improving employee performance by a similar amount, your organization can produce or grow at a 5 percent greater level without adding any additional people. This is a worthwhile annual goal for any manager!

Should a manager promote someone who has a history of just meeting expectations and whose promotional potential is questionable? Yes, of course! There is nothing substandard about just doing your job, and every promotion is a gamble of sorts. Companies too often consider only those employees who seem outstanding as candidates for promotion. They overlook the fact that because the majority of people are working below the level at which they could perform, there is always plenty of room for additional or new responsibilities. Most promotions go to individuals who get the job done without any heroics or all-star performances.

Handling Employees in the Possible-Retention Subcategory

Employees who are not performing to expectations may be new hires, newly promoted individuals, or people whose performance was once satisfactory but has dropped. Their failures or shortcomings should be thoroughly documented, with specific issues or critical incidents outlined and dates included.

This rating suggests that with additional coaching or training, the employee can reach the desired level of performance within a reasonable period—perhaps the time it would take to find and train or introduce a replacement employee.

This employee should be in some form of documented corrective action program that has identified the problem areas and contains required performance levels and time frames. You have a duty to others who are performing adequately to maintain the existing job standards for this employee. Don't remove elements of the job. Someone else will have to do them or they will go undone. Also, removing elements will subvert your goal of improving overall personnel utilization in the organization; instead, it maintains or accommodates poor performers.

It is good practice to refuse to transfer any employee who is going through a corrective action program. Some managers feel that if the employee were placed in another job, he or she would find his or her calling and become a valued contributor. But all a transfer really does is shuffle the problem around until it falls in the lap of a serious manager. And by then, considerable time and money have been wasted.

Another practice that will help you maintain expected standards of performance is to allow only one "possible retention" rating per employee. The second time, the rating is changed to "not retainable" and the employee is handled on the basis of that evaluation rating. The second chance everyone deserves was the first "possible retention" period of corrective action. As Andy Rooney says, "Did you ever notice how the same things keep happening to the same people?"

When you evaluate corrective action progress, be aware that some level of improvement will almost always occur. Don't overreact when you see some progress. If it isn't quite enough, it isn't enough. If you accept it, you are, in effect, lowering the standards of performance for everyone in the department or company. Explain this to the employee when the corrective action process begins. It is surprising how many people are allowed to perform at levels that require their managers to ignore critical performance issues. These people often will come to life for the first manager who talks about the possibility of their termination. Marginal performers owe the company a fair day's work. If they don't provide that, the company expects its managers to react firmly and quickly.

Handling Employees Who Are Not Retainable

This evaluation implies that the employee will be terminated for failure to perform to the job's stated expectations or requirements or to meet specific business plan–related objectives. Other types of terminations, such as reductions in force and violations of company policy, should be handled in a different manner. Also, any attendance or punctuality issues should always be dealt with as they occur, not postponed until the performance evaluation meeting.

If an employee is not retainable, start the termination process at the evaluation meeting. You already know that the employee has little chance of continuing in her or his current job; an employee on a corrective action program or in a probationary period should also not be surprised by a negative review. In fact, both parties should go into the meeting expecting the same outcome. Both should have been talking, measuring, and monitoring progress with clear indications of areas where performance improvements had to occur and what the consequences for failure to improve would be. This process should have been carefully documented to substantiate any decision to terminate

Knowing that the employee has failed to meet the job's expectations or objectives, you should assume that, unless something unexpected comes up during the evaluation meeting, the employee has to be terminated. The only other alternative is transfer to a lesser or different job, if an appropriate one exists.

No further corrective action or coaching effort will do any good at this point. Neither will lowering standards. An employee's failure to perform never justifies lowering any expectations or requirements, especially if they have been documented in a corrective action format and agreed to by both parties. The expectations and objectives have to remain the same throughout the corrective action or probationary period. Don't change the rules or the goal line just because someone is losing. Do the employee a favor and release him or her to find a better use of his or her skills or talents. Offer outplacement services, if appropriate; process the severance payment where applicable; and begin the process of selecting a replacement so that you can get back to your primary responsibility: selecting and managing competent employees.

Using a Management Review Board to Ensure Consistent Evaluations

Even when a company chooses to administer and apply a performance evaluation program or to process evaluations consistently at every level of its organization, it cannot leave the process entirely in the hands of its managers. But no matter what the state of a performance evaluation program, it's a good idea to have a "gatekeeper" who continually reviews the performance evaluation process in the organization.

A gatekeeper can audit the process to make sure that standards are being enforced and maintained, even by reluctant or renegade managers. Often this responsibility falls on the human resources person or department. Ideally, this monitoring not only ensures that reviews are held on schedule, but also tracks the talent that exists within the company and how it is being managed and utilized—an aspect overlooked by too many companies. To monitor the process and provide a forum to review the utilization of the organization's human resources talent, some companies create a management review board. This board is made up of several members of upper management whose function is to:

1. Ensure that any and all scheduled performance evaluation reviews are conducted on time and in an appropirate manner. The board does this by meeting monthly to compare the scheduled review list against the actual reviews conducted.
2. Identify and study any performance evaluations that warrant attention in terms of their impact on the organization's human resources needs, based on the review board's information about the future goals and direction of the company.

Through this process, exceptional performers are noted, consistency is studied, and managers who are not doing an adequate job of evaluating or managing their people are identified. In smaller organizations, in which the members of this management review board have daily contact with most employees, the board can identify managers who may be inflating or ignoring performance issues. There can be more than one such board in an organization; a department, function, or division can establish a review board to keep its own house in order.

The main benefit of the review board is that it ensures that all levels of management will take their responsibility for managing performance seriously and that it oversees the process and ensures that the maximum effort is being made by everyone.

PART FOUR
Reward

Most employees express little concern about or interest in selection, direction, or evaluation, but everyone is interested in rewards. Employees want rewards. Companies reward results. Not effort, not ability—just results. That's because results in the form of company profits are the key to a company's future.

The challenge to management is to match the proper people and rewards with the desired results. While it is not meant to be a highly detailed analysis of compensation and reward programs, this section will make you aware of the elements, advantages, and disadvantages of various reward systems so that you can use them to attract, select, and reward people who can help your department and your company produce the results they need if they are to succeed.

CHAPTER 10

The Purpose of Rewards

What is a reward?

A reward is whatever somebody has coming as a result of his or her performance. It may be something positive like a promotion or a raise, or something negative like a demotion, a transfer, or termination.

That's different from compensation. Compensation, of course, is what people get for putting in time on the job: money. While some rewards are monetary, many are not.

Many people see the company's loyalty as a reward. When a plant closes after decades in the same community, people say, "I've worked here for twenty years and they closed down the plant. What kind of reward is that?" Others find rewards in a job they can walk or bicycle to, or a schedule that lets them be with their children. Engineers and computer programmers who are not interested in becoming managers are rewarded by an alternative career path that lets them focus on their craft. Professional athletes are rewarded by the celebrity that goes with playing with the elite. And postal carriers and military personnel are rewarded with the opportunity to retire early with a secure pension.

In a sense, compensation is the system that delivers rewards to employees. A well-thought-out compensation program is designed to deliver rewards that attract and retain the kind of workforce a company needs if it is to reach its goals. For some companies, the best compensation program is fixed; in others, compensation is based upon performance. But whether rewards are fixed or variable, their purpose is to generate certain activities and results by motivating people to maximize their individual efforts.

Every reward system costs money—whether it is base pay, bonuses, commissions, benefits, time off, unpaid leaves, cafeterias, parking spaces, soft chairs, mountain views, or a manager's taking extra time to work with and understand an employee. The only rewards that don't cost anything are the rewards that employees give themselves: loyalty, extra effort, cordial working relationships with other employees, showing up during bad weather, and showing respect for a supervisor even though the employee may not always agree with him or her.

These "free" rewards are all derived from an employee's attitude. A company's reward system can do little to change an employee's attitude. But it can affect individual employee performance.

On the surface, attitude and performance seem tightly linked. Ask early morning commuters at the train station if they are looking forward to spending the day at work, and most of them will say that there are plenty of other places that they would rather be spending the day. Bad attitude! But ask if they will give the company a good and fair effort that day, and most will say they always have and always will. Ask them, further, if, should things at work require extra effort, they will give that extra effort. Most, again, will say that they of course will do whatever it takes. Great performance!

Even though their attitude may tilt more toward staying home than toward going to work, most workers will give an occasional extra effort without an increase in rewards. But if you try to get it every day, when it was not required before, you will be disappointed in a short time. Unless, of course, management changes the reward system to compensate the employees for the extra performance.

Rewards: An Integral Part of Selection

Reward systems vary, and the system used needs to be matched to the employees and the goals of the organization. Consider two identical production facilities, Facility A and Facility B. In Facility A you install a reward system in which, at the beginning of the year, everyone is paid everything that they have coming to them for that entire year of work. In Facility B you install a reward system that is based on output, with the rewards paid on a weekly basis. Depending on whether they perform above or below the standards, Facility B people can earn as much as one and a half times or as little as half of what Facility A people earn.

When you begin hiring staff for the two facilities, you let each person you hire choose which facility to work in on the basis of how the person wants to be rewarded. The people who select Facility A will be different from the people who select Facility B, because people have different comfort levels and are willing to accept different degrees of risk to their income.

Obviously, the selection process and the reward system are directly tied to the level of performance the organization will receive. If you hire Facility A types to work under a Facility B–type reward system, the aggressive performance you expect may never materialize, and if it does, it will not be sustained. Hire Facility B types into a Facility A–type reward program and you *will* get Facility A performance—from people who feel frustrated because their energy is not being utilized. Change the reward system to a Facility B type and performance will increase.

The moral? If you want certain levels of performance over certain periods of time, you need to design the reward system to appeal to the types of people you need in order to get the performance you want. Some of the rules that guide this principle are:

(1)   Proper selection + proper rewards = desired performance

(2)   Improper selection + proper rewards = less than desired performance + turnover

(3)   Proper selection + improper rewards = erratic performance + turnover

The message is that neither selection nor reward stands alone in terms of producing the performance required. The best organizations link both of these elements when they determine their hiring practices and pay programs.

Focusing on Time and Cost When Rewarding Employees

The military is the only organization that can operate without being highly focused on the linkage between selection and pay and performance. It can operate with a different set of rules.

There are two reasons the military can manage like this. Unlike a company and its management, the military does not have to make a profit, and it will never go out of business. And although both the military and business need performance in order to meet their objectives, the performance the military expects is not the same kind of performance that private industry expects.

The military is designed to discover and destroy; business is designed to develop and distribute. A military unit may wander around the countryside for days without ever finding or running into the enemy. It needs food and fuel while it searches. When it eventually discovers the enemy, it may face them for additional days, waiting for the weather to clear before attacking or defending itself. While it waits, it still needs food and fuel. Unproductive time, and the cost associated, means little to the military.

Business, on the other hand, can seldom absorb unproductive time and costs for long. A business has to begin distribution as quickly as possible in order to recoup its investment and cover its costs. If the military rushed out onto the battlefield and started to fight as soon as it saw the enemy, its chances of survival would be greatly reduced. If business waited until the competition showed itself before developing advanced products, and then waited until the competition started selling before it began distribution, its chances of success would be reduced.

The key difference between these two organizations is time and cost versus programs. Business has to worry about the time involved and the cost incurred; the military relies on strategies or programs that have been historically tested and will be used no matter what the time or cost. The military practices and drills many of the same routines over and over in order to be prepared. Business relies more on continual change to stay alive.

Business managers have to continually work at shortening the time and reducing the costs involved in the way they operate. When it comes to managing people, that means being as efficient as possible in the selection, direction, evaluation, and reward of their employees. In the simplest terms, being as efficient as possible, keeping time and cost to a minimum, means one thing: getting it right the first time! That means selecting the proper people to begin with and rewarding them in a way that fits their work ethic and workload so that turnover is low and the company gets the performance—meaning time and cost—it needs.

Companies should realize that people working for them stay there because the system of rewards suits their personalities. It is counterproductive for a company that wants to improve employee performance to try to achieve that goal by simply designing or buying a different reward program. People are not going to change their performance just because the company changed the pay program. In fact, a new program is more likely to result in increased turnover than improved performance. Employees confronting the new system are sure to complain and may eventually leave. Companies facing such complaints often switch back to the original pay program in order to accommodate employees and prevent turnover.

A company that wants different performance and wants to reward specific performance levels will probably need to employ different types of people. It will not have to replace everyone, but it certainly will have to endure a significant amount of turnover. That's because an organization has a culture, and no organization can change its culture without changing the type of people who work there. Companies do not have the hundreds or thousands of years that nations or tribes can devote to establishing a culture. They have to do it over the weekend. If a company needs a certain type of performance, it will have to hire a certain type of person. And that type of person will generally produce best under a certain kind of reward system.

That is why you cannot install a reward system until you

can clearly define the performance you want. The most popular reward program in the civilized world may not induce the performance your company or function or department requires.

Start by focusing on time and costs instead of reward programs. Then design the reward system that will best induce that required performance. Next, determine what types of people are likely to function the best under that reward program, and select new hires on that basis.

This commonsense approach requires awareness, planning, and discipline, all of which take time. Many firms define jobs clearly and conduct compatibility and skills tests as part of the selection process. They design reward systems that are tightly linked to the performance the firm needs. They find time for these practices either because the top person in the company states that it will be done that way, or because after an individual manager begins to do this, it catches on in other parts of the company because it produces better results. If performance and getting it right the first time are high enough on your list of objectives, you will find the time to design a reward program that works.

Developing and Installing a Base-Pay System

Most managers have more control over compensation than they do over rewards—especially rewards like where the business is located and how many and what kind of jobs it offers. Customers and the marketplace determine these factors. Managers *can* design compensation programs and determine whether they offer base pay, variable pay, or a combination thereof. Secondary compensation programs such as gain sharing can be added to the traditional base pay programs to create a set of programs directed at specific people and company objectives.

The most basic reward in business is base pay—the set amount an employee earns per hour, week, or month. In a base pay program, a salary range is established for each job classification. This range is determined, for the most part, by how much other companies pay for similar jobs. That range moves up, and occasionally down, primarily for two reasons: the effect of the annual pay increases that most companies grant to their employees, and the practice of lateral hiring, or bringing in a new hire to perform the same job he or she was doing at another company. In this situation, the hiring firm pays a premium to get that person to leave her or his current company and join the new one—a premium that ratchets up the average rate paid for that type of job more than the normal annual increases would.

From a labor cost standpoint, it is better to hire people who, when they join your company, will be receiving what amounts to a promotion in responsibilities. For example, if instead of hiring a senior buyer for a senior buyer opening, you hire someone who was an experienced buyer at another company, you will pay less than what veteran senior buyers are making in the marketplace. But if you hire a senior buyer, you will pay a premium to get that person to move into a lateral senior buyer job at your company. You'll end up paying more than the market for that position.

As a manager, it's your job to protect company assets, including payroll. If you are unfamiliar with how base pay is determined by the economy and the labor market, you will not be able to determine whether you are getting the most value for those payroll dollars, especially when it's time to reward performance. Too many managers simply think in terms of giving annual increases instead of considering increases in the context of the company's internal and external labor market. That's why it is important to understand how a base pay structure is constructed.

As companies grow, they advertise for and hire employees at whatever pay level it takes to get the people they feel they need at the time. As the company matures, it may establish its own set of pay ranges for the different types of jobs in the company. A pay range consists of a minimum or entry rate and a maximum or highest amount that will be paid for the specific job at that company. One way in which small or growing companies get into trouble is by failing to set pay range maximums for job classifications.

Just as there is a price range for materials such as steel, wood, paper, and plastics, so is there a price range for jobs. If no limits are established, a company can find itself paying more for labor than the market or its competition is paying. Continuing to grant significant pay increases to employees whose responsibilities have not changed for years will make a company less than competitive in terms of labor costs. But setting maximum salary amounts benefits companies in two ways.

First, it prevents the company from paying more than the market for a set of skills or a common job. Without limits, an employee who receives annual increases for the same job for ten years may earn 25 to 50 percent more than the average high end for that job in the market. This, in turn, creates upward pressure on pay levels for other employees or jobs in that organization. But when ceilings are in place, employees who hit the maximum can earn more only by increasing their skills and taking on more responsibilities—in essence, by performing a higher-level job that makes them worth more money to the company.

Second, establishing pay range maximums for jobs creates healthy employee turnover. Healthy turnover is brought about when an employee reaches the maximum of the range, realizes that he or she will no longer receive substantial pay increases, and, if no promotions are available, leaves for another job. It permits the company to go outside and hire another person at a lower pay rate. Not only does this type of turnover keep labor costs from getting ahead of the going rate for jobs, but it also brings fresh ideas and approaches to the company.

Pay range maximums for jobs that can be compared to similar or identical jobs at other companies are generally based on the outside job market. By gathering information on what other companies pay for such benchmark jobs as bookkeepers, buyers, data entry clerks, and janitors—jobs that are basically the same in every company and industry—a company can develop a set of pay ranges that is representative of the outside or external market. In this way, the company establishes equity with the external market.

Organizations also need to set maximum pay rates for jobs that are unique and cannot reliably be compared to similar jobs in other companies. When external information is not available, you need to establish internal equity to set a fair pay scale.

Internal equity is simply the relative importance, value, or skill requirements of jobs inside the company. If there are three jobs that are closely comparable to a benchmark job in terms of importance, value, and skill, you can assume that those three nonbenchmark jobs are worth and should be paid the same as the benchmark job. This establishes internal equity for those four positions. By evaluating all the jobs in the organization and grouping around benchmark jobs, you can identify their market pay levels.

Sometimes supply and demand causes a company to exceed its salary ceilings. If the demand for workers who can fill a certain type of job is significantly greater than the supply, a company may have to pay a premium for those workers until balance is again created in the market. A manager or company has to avoid moving a job affected by unusual market pressures into a higher pay range than is dictated by the evaluation process. The evaluation process is a way to determine internal equity that has little to do with the market. To move the job because of a shift in external supply and demand distorts this internal job-to-job comparison and could lead to long-term internal wage cost excesses.

Besides establishing pay ranges, a base salary program designates job classifications. A list of all jobs within a typical organization in order of importance, value, or skill might begin with chief executive officer and end with something like mailroom clerk. Dividing this list into ranges of pay and evaluation groups is not thorough enough. Federal overtime laws, internal accounting requirements, and general payroll administration practices require that jobs be further grouped into several distinctive job classifications, depending on the size and type of organization. Under the Fair Labor Standards Act, workers in "nonexempt" jobs have to be paid overtime; those in "exempt" jobs do not because they are exempt from that set of laws. Those two categories are as follows:

Nonexempt (Overtime Required)	*Exempt (Overtime Not Required)*
Direct labor (or hourly)	Professional
Clerical (or office)	Middle management
Skilled trades	Top management

A company setting up a base pay structure needs to carefully observe these laws, especially in the clerical and professional classifications. These are generally the greatest problem areas when it comes to back pay settlements and penalties that result from employee complaints to government agencies.

Merit Pay or Automatic Rewards: Which Is More Appropriate?

There are really only two base-pay formats available to the management of any organization: merit pay and automatic rewards. These two formats determine the manner in which management grants rewards or pay increases affecting the base-pay rates of employees.

Merit increase programs are designed to reward employees for individual performance. Two different employees performing the same job for the same amount of time and earning the same base-pay rate could receive different increase amounts if their supervisor could justify it. Depending on the parameters the supervisor applied, one person could get a 6 percent pay increase, the other a 3 percent increase. Besides rewarding results, merit increase programs can reward attitude, attendance, and other factors, although it's best to keep the focus on individual performance and extra effort.

Automatic progression programs relate base pay to the length of time someone has held a job. A typical schedule might be: Hire rate, $9.50/hour; after 3 months, $9.80/hour; after 6 months, $10.10/hour; after 1 year, $10.60/hour; after 2 years, $11.15/hour; after 3 years, $11.70/hour. This type of schedule usually stops at three years.

The philosophy behind automatic progression programs is that employees who are doing the same job and performing that job satisfactorily should be paid the same for their skills. Because the only distinction it makes is length of time on the job, it emphasizes performance to minimum job requirements, and places no value on above-expectations performance.

Every base-pay program is either merit or automatic progression in its basic design. Because the cost of labor under the two types of program is similar, program cost is not a significant factor in selecting one over the other. Which one to choose depends on two issues:

1. Can and should management base its rewards on the fact that some individuals do a better job than others, or is that extra effort of little value to the company?
2. If management does base rewards on individual performance levels, can management effectively administer that type of program?

The first issue is partly a philosophical one and partly a function of the jobs, or employee groups, being considered. The second is a very practical one in that it involves the amount of training and administration the company's management personnel can be given and can handle. To understand why companies might select one type of program over the other, or to make that decision for an organization or operation, a manager has to be aware of and understand the advantages and disadvantages of each type, which are summarized in Exhibit 10-1.

How Merit and Automatic Progression Programs Affect Employee Groups

Merit reward programs are almost universally used for exempt groups, such as professionals, middle management, and top management, and for the majority of nonexempt office or clerical job groups. They can also be used for skilled trades and direct labor or hourly production jobs. They are not used in unionized operations, or where unionization is a potential threat. Few unions accept merit pay programs because unions sell the concept that everyone who is doing the same job must be treated the same, seniority being the only exception.

Automatic progression is hardly ever used for exempt job groups and seldom for office or clerical groups. It is overwhelmingly used for skilled trades and direct labor or hourly produc-

Exhibit 10-1. Summary of the advantages and disadvantages of the merit reward and automatic progression programs.

Merit Reward Program

Advantages	*Disadvantages*
❑ Allows greater freedom in rewarding extra skill of and effort from individual employees	❑ Allows for favoritism and inconsistencies in reward application
❑ Gives better performance feedback to employees	❑ Requires format for objective performance evaluation by supervisor
❑ Provides for more focused use of reward dollars	❑ Requires managers who can deal with the judgment and communication associated with the required evaluation process
❑ Places managers in an active role in the management of the people within the function they are responsible for	

Automatic Progression Program

Advantages	*Disadvantages*
❑ More consistent in terms of time and amount	❑ Does not recognize extra effort or marginal performance
❑ Does not require recorded evaluations for performance that meets expectations	❑ Reduces the emphasis on the performance evaluation exercise
❑ Relieves management of considerable administrative requirements and judgment calls on performance rewards	❑ Eliminates valuable face-to-face evaluation and general performance discussions between supervisor and employee

---

tion groups and is the prevalent method contained in union contracts.

Depending on its needs, an organization might have every employee group on a merit program; have the direct labor (hourly) on automatic progression and everyone else on merit; have the direct labor and skilled trades on automatic progression, with the rest on merit; or have all nonexempt groups on automatic progression and exempt groups on merit.

Rewarding Performance With Merit and Automatic Progression Programs

A merit program makes it easy to reward the above-expectations performer with a reward or increase that is greater than those granted to others who are performing at lower levels. That's not possible in the automatic progression system, unless the program is designed with specific progression steps that are not linked to time. In that case, a manager could skip an above-expectations performer over the next scheduled step in the progression and award a higher base rate, or move the person to the next progression step at an earlier date. It all depends on how rigidly the program is administered and the justification supplied by the manager.

A merit program makes it easy for a timid manager to deal with an employee whose performance is below expectations. By giving the poorly performing employee a smaller reward amount, the manager can simultaneously reward performance and make the point that that performance is less than expected. But this creates two problems. First, although the employee was rewarded, he or she is probably unhappy; second, the company suffers from having an underperforming employee who believes that he or she will continue to be rewarded for that level of output. The correct procedure would be to set up a time period for the improvement, then hold up any increase until performance has reached the level expected. Anything else costs the company money.

People who are performing below expectations in an automatic progression program are supposed to be held back instead of being moved to the next scheduled step. If a reward is not held up, a manager can expect a reaction from the peers of the employee who is performing poorly. Employees know who isn't performing. When poor performance is condoned, the standard of performance for everyone may drop. Why should anyone work harder than anyone else when each will get the same increase amount? A manager will eventually have to face up to the poor performers in order to maintain the required output from the rest of the employee group.

Performance Evaluation and Merit or Automatic Progression Programs

Formal performance evaluation is an essential part of any program that grants pay increase rewards to employees. Typically, a merit reward program requires more details, time, and effort on the part of the manager than an automatic program. Any manager who makes performance distinctions among employees in his or her department needs written justification to support those distinctions. Written evaluations are often required by management further up the chain for reasons of control, and they are certainly necessary in order to defend the company against unfair employment practices charges filed by employees.

The automatic progression program, on the other hand, can function well without any formal evaluation record for those employees who move through the pay progression at the prescribed speed. A performance evaluation record is required only for exceptions in terms of level or time. A manager who chooses to hold an employee's scheduled increase back would have to justify that decision in writing. So would a manager who wanted someone to skip a level or move up in a shorter period of time.

Normal increases require no justification and serve as an evaluation because they tell the employee that he or she is performing up to expectations. But therein lies a problem: The manager and the employee could go for years without having a formal or structured discussion about that employee's career with the company or performance in the job. Almost everyone likes to talk to the boss occasionally about how things are going. The quick and easy approach to performance evaluation provided by an automatic progression system makes it too easy to forgo these important face-to-face meetings.

Pay Grade Ranges and Merit vs. Automatic Increases

While a merit increase system can operate without pay grade ranges—the merit increase amounts can simply be applied to the base pay without any concern for ranges—it is better to have ranges in place in order to control the maximum amounts paid. Without a cap, as was mentioned earlier, the salaries of good or very good performers can quickly soar to levels well above the job market rate, placing the company in an uncompetitive position relative to the market and its competitors in terms of labor costs.

By definition, automatic progression programs require employees to move through a series of specific pay levels. The progression steps constitute the range for that job or group of jobs. This progression stream has to stop somewhere, usually at three or five years, and that last level becomes the maximum of the range.

Withholding Rewards

When a company is faced with a slowdown in orders or a similar problem, it may have to freeze its labor costs for a short period of time. That may mean eliminating or curtailing the granting of pay increases to employees. While the company can certainly do this regardless of what type of reward program is in place, it is harder to implement in an automatic progression system.

The principle behind automatic progression is that an employee who has been in a job a specified amount of time will be or should be rewarded with the next higher level of pay. The employee gets the message that he or she has earned this reward based on time and performance. To back away from that commitment can create misunderstandings and resentment on the part of the affected employees. Also, once the freeze is lifted, the employees' length of service and their respective pay rates relative to the progression steps will not agree. A company can expect pressure to make adjustments once things improve.

A merit program, on the other hand, does not spell out any specific amounts of increase or any exact times for increases. The only real commitment in a merit program is to a scheduled performance evaluation, at which time the individual's pay level and its potential for adjustment are to be considered. That commitment can be met even if, because of a company wage freeze, no increases are granted at that time. In the automatic progression program, an increase is seen as almost guaranteed if the employee just does the job; the merit program has no such obvious guarantee.

The merit program also allows small or token increases instead of none at all. In the automatic progression this is not as easy, although it is possible to redefine the progression steps at amounts lower than those previously published.

Regardless of the type of program in place, wage freezes are easiest to administer if they last for a complete year and affect everyone in the company. To freeze salaries of part of the employee group means that once increases are restarted, adjustments will have to be made to those who experienced the freeze in order to maintain internal equity among employee reward levels. Obviously, going back and granting increases that were denied because of a wage freeze eliminates any saving achieved during that freeze.

CHAPTER 11

Variable-Reward and Nonpay-Reward Programs

If base-pay–reward programs are the family sedans of business, variable-reward programs are the sports cars. These are far more complex than base-pay programs and much more challenging. They can create excitement and change attitudes if they are designed to get you to your destination. They require extra care and maintenance, but they will return more than your investment in terms of ongoing benefits.

A variable-reward program can maximize individual effort by motivating people to focus on certain activities and generate desirable results. While people in the workplace are motivated by many different factors, a significant percentage are motivated by money. By creating variable monetary rewards, management can motivate some types of people to make greater efforts than they would if they were simply paid a base or fixed wage. This is the principle behind variable rewards.

The appropriateness and eventual success of variable rewards depends on the degree of control that an individual or group has over job elements. Variable rewards are not appropriate and will seldom work when a job is very rigid and structured and its outcome is predictable. But variable rewards make sense for jobs with little structure whose occupants are free to direct their own work within a broad framework of activities.

The success of a variable-reward program also depends on

the type of employee working within the reward system. Installing a variable-reward program and applying it to people with the wrong personalities will probably produce some improvements in output, but not for long. In the end, the program may create more problems than benefits. You need to match individuals with the desired behavior traits to the appropriate rewards. Neither behavior nor reward stands on its own.

Variable rewards provide focus. Whenever an element of a job is assigned a specific reward, that element will be the focus of the employee's attention. Usually the element assigned such a reward is one that is unlikely to improve in quality or quantity without additional attention. For example, gain-sharing programs direct employee attention to improvements in processes and reductions in costs. When people are rewarded for devising better ways to perform daily, almost automatic tasks, improved efficiencies occur. And when they are asked to restructure the way they use company supplies, equipment, and other resources, costs are directly affected. These small but important issues might never be given serious attention if management did not focus on them through the gain-sharing concept, which shares the savings with the employees.

Why Managers Don't Like Variable Rewards

Variable-reward programs like gain sharing often are not installed simply because management believes they are difficult to design, are time-consuming to install, take too long to pay off, or will be misunderstood or resisted by the present employee group. And indeed, employees often react negatively when variable-reward programs are proposed or introduced, because they were hired into and are accustomed to a fixed base-pay system that pays more for presence than for performance. When that system is threatened, no wonder they object! Short-term, all of this can seem too disruptive to the operation. As a result, the idea or effort is dropped.

That's too bad—because even though they take months to produce results, in the appropriate situations and with the appropriate personnel, variable-reward programs produce better results. But often management considers only the growing pains and doesn't take the time to measure the benefits of the transition. Also, management themselves may not be on a variable-compensation program, and may not really want to be. This brings us back to the initial selection process. Managers who are not risk takers shy away from placing any of their pay at risk or linking it to results. And they especially do not want to link it to the results of others.

Many managers do not want to be put on an objectives-driven variable-reward program designed to complement a traditional base-pay format. They argue that things change too fast for managers to be held to objectives that were set months back, and that this will divert attention away from the teamwork required. Instead, they want to be awarded bonuses based on annual company profit. This is fine if the company as a whole has made or exceeded its profit targets—but it does little to improve the effectiveness of individual managers.

Teams that win the World Series or the Super Bowl divide the rewards among their players, but that doesn't mean that everyone on those teams performed equally well. The team did well, but it could have done better if certain individuals had performed better. This is why even top teams replace players. Desired or acceptable overall performance does not mean that individual performance should be ignored.

Variable rewards deserve a place in every organization, and every organization needs people who react positively to the opportunities presented under these types of programs. Still, variable rewards can be misapplied. Paying astronauts by the mile probably will not affect the distance traveled in a lunar mission; astronauts will still take the most direct route instead of detouring around Mars. But on earth, that basis of payment does make for some long cab rides.

Using Variable Rewards to Acknowledge Group and Individual Efforts

The first step in designing an appropriate variable-reward system is to determine whether it should apply to groups or to individuals. The answer depends upon whether the greatest degree of control or influence rests with the individual or the group. A room full of telemarketers would respond to an individual-performance-based reward program; a team of employees responsible for installing a large, four-color printing press would respond better to a group reward program.

The program doesn't have to be one or the other. Many companies offer employees a combination of individual and group variable-reward programs. And most of these companies also compensate those same people with a base-pay wage. This may seem like a complicated administrative and accounting exercise, but in most companies the basic elements are already being measured. It is a matter of taking these measurements a step further and transforming them into pay amounts.

The ideal combination program would give an employee a minimum amount in the form of a base wage that is paid regardless of job assignments or performance—assuming, of course, that the employee does not exhibit any performance problems. The segment of the job that depends on the employee's individual effort would be tied to a payout when effort resulted in better-than-expected output. A third part of the employee's reward would be based on the results produced by whatever group or team that person functions in. To design a combination program for your company, start with this broad-scope application of rewards and work back to an appropriate mix.

Companies that offer these three forms of rewards for each employee group or classification know that, while some people are upset when the total compensation distributed varies, most employees take pride and see the challenge in working within this type of system. Their company culture reflects that and generally does not accept individuals who do not take pride in maximizing their personal contributions.

Using Variable Rewards to Increase Quality

Variable rewards need not be strictly tied to the volume of a product produced. They can also reinforce the quality of the product or service, or customer satisfaction.

Several variable-reward formats are linked directly to quality and customer satisfaction issues. The broadest type of variable-reward program, companywide profit sharing, obviously reflects these two issues, because few companies would make a profit if their product or service did not provide acceptable levels of quality. Annual division bonus programs are also based on those same market demands. Gain sharing, which rewards for efficiencies, also requires reductions in scrap and rework costs if variable rewards are to be received.

If a company, function, or department assigns individual or group objectives, those objectives should include standards that reflect the quality and service parameters required to receive rewards upon completion. Individual piecework and sales commission programs—the oldest and still most widely used forms of variable rewards—always outline appropriate quality and service levels. Another way to get the best quality is to link quality targets to an individual or group reward program. If management pays for acceptable product instead of hours worked, the quality of the output will be directly affected. Management needs to take the time to think through the job elements and to design the proper tasks and processes.

Quality was one of the biggest problems faced by the management of the Apollo space program. In the spacecraft that would take three men to the moon and, with luck, return them to earth, there were tens of thousands of parts that had to work if the mission was to succeed. Each of these individual parts had to have a reliability rating of 0.99999, or only one failure in 100,000 tests. There wasn't any way to subject each of those tens of thousands of parts to this kind of testing and still complete the mission within the decade.

Instead of using this as a reason to change the project deadline, the management made a bold decision. The project engineers told them that it wasn't necessary to test all those parts to that degree of reliability. Most of these engineers took the view that if an individual part was designed right and built to specifications, it would work as designed every time. Engineers and management felt that time and money would be better spent searching for design flaws rather than mindlessly testing parts.

The same logic applies to reward programs. If the time is

spent in the design stage, the program will work. In the variable-reward arena, the design includes selecting the right kind of people and installing the right kind of reward program. When that happens, the results will be there, in terms of both output quality and quantity.

Selecting and Installing a Variable-Reward Program

In evaluating a variable-reward program, many managers have two questions:

1. Just how much more output will I get if I use a form of variable reward?
2. I feel that I'm already paying employees to give me their best efforts. Why should I have to reward them with more money to get what I should already be receiving?

The first question is hard to answer because it calls for comparisons with similar companies and their experiences—and even this research will not provide a reliable set of exact numbers. The best thing you can do is design a program you feel should work, administer it in a manner that champions the concepts, and continue to evaluate it to determine its future.

The second question reveals the manager's mind-set. Managers who always give their best efforts often assume that all employees should feel and act the same way. Some do, but some don't. There is a vast group that gives a fair day's work for a fair day's pay, but seldom more. By becoming management, individuals have shown that they have a particular approach to work, education, risk, and willingness to assume responsibilities for the performance of others.

People who choose not to join the management ranks have a different value system. They may select the skilled trades or professions for the security they provide, or they may stay in the hourly or clerical ranks because they have chosen to forgo the challenge of further education. Whatever the reasons, not everybody gives his or her all, or even a little more than is necessary, in a job. Managers cannot expect the attitude they themselves exhibit to exist in the majority of others; if it did, everyone would be potential management material.

Don't assume that everyone else is continually giving that extra effort. They aren't. It may seem offensive to have to distribute additional rewards in order to generate extra effort from employees, but it's the results that count, not your personal prejudices. Very few managers get promoted because they refuse to consider, or apply, options or alternatives. And variable-reward programs are very powerful when they are directed at the vast majority of people who give a day's work for a day's pay.

Variable rewards can range from the piecework application in small operations to the profit-sharing programs of many larger companies. Let's look at the types of programs that individual managers need to be familiar with and understand.

Management Bonuses

Bonus rewards to management personnel are an essential part of any variable-reward program. Their presence is usually the driving force behind the incremental, above-average success of companies that lead their industry, field, or market segment. These types of rewards focus on managers and highlight the specific areas on which the company places its emphasis. They are as much a method for directing the management group as for rewarding it.

The most common issue in designing and administering management bonus programs is deciding where to draw the line between performance that is directly influenced by the individual manager's actions and that resulting from the actions of the entire company's management team. This problem is at the heart of the distribution of reward dollars.

If a company has generated a pool of profit dollars to distribute among its managers, it has to determine who will get how much. There are three basic methods that it can use to do this:

1. It can simply grant an equal dollar amount to each manager eligible for the distribution. But unless all eligible managers

are at the same level in the organization, this approach results in lower-level managers receiving bonuses that are larger relative to their base pay than those of high-level, and higher-paid, managers. This is not a very fair or a very motivating method.

2. It can divide the bonus pool by the total payroll amount of management base salaries and then distribute that percentage to each manager. For example, say there is $15,000 in a bonus pool for two managers. One makes $50,000; the other $100,000. Thus, $15,000 is 10 percent of the total payroll of $150,000. A 10 percent bonus for manager number one is $5,000; 10 percent for manager number two is $10,000. Each gets the same percentage but a different dollar amount.

3. In this method, management positions at each level in the organization receive a specific percentage of their base salary. In other words, managers reporting directing to the top executive or owner may be eligible for a reward amount equal to 25 percent of their base salary; those at the level just below may be eligible for 15 percent; those at the next level, for 5 percent, and so on. Percentages may change from year to year depending on the number of management levels and the size of the bonus pool. This concept is understandable and easy to communicate, and it addresses the issue that higher-level managers feel that their impact on the success of the operation is more significant than that of lower-level contributors.

A fourth method, and one of the most popular, is the discretionary reward method, in which the person in charge simply uses his or her own judgment to determine how much each manager deserves. No formula is established or communicated to the eligible managers. In fact, the managers may not even know that they are eligible until the rewards are actually distributed.

Determining which formula to use to distribute rewards is only one issue that arises when developing a management bonus program. Chapter 12 will address this and other issues concerning management bonus programs.

Commissions to Salespeople

Sales commission programs almost always involve variable rewards. These programs offer the greatest opportunities for imagination and creativity on the part of management. Often these opportunities also become the reasons for a program's downfall. The main objective of any sales reward program has to be the generation of profitable sales levels and amounts for the company. After that, the emphasis should be on creating an understandable and credible format that salespeople feel comfortable operating under. Creating a plan full of gimmicks and controls that excite management but discourage the sales staff means that management has lost sight of the true objective of any variable-reward program: to motivate employees—in this case, the sales staff—to pursue the same goals and objectives as management.

In some companies, salespeople are faced with the possibility that as their performance or sales increase, their reward program will be changed in a way that will lessen their commission earnings or even cap them once they reach a certain level. The companies that practice these types of actions are not administering reward programs; they are operating programs that penalize good performance!

There are other ways in which companies penalize good sales performers that do not directly involve the compensation program but do affect the reward systems. One way is to redistrict territories. If a salesperson is earning at a level that some sales manager feels is excessive, that manager may simply shrink or change that salesperson's territory, thereby making it harder for that person to earn as much in commissions. The thinking behind this kind of action is slippery, at best.

A company that changes the commission reward program every time salespeople begin to earn at levels that the company feels are excessive is often operating on the assumption that people will back off in their efforts if they become too comfortable. This may be true of some people, but not of genuine sales types. If management has selected the right types of people for the sales staff, this fear is unfounded. And if the reward program is designed correctly to begin with—meaning that the reward payouts are factored into the cost of doing business, leaving enough dollars for profit—there should be no reason to change it. If management changes a program in order to increase profits, it will reap increased turnover or apathy among the sales force, not increased profits.

A cap on sales commission payouts also results in turnover and apathy—and eventually, a cap on sales.

Gain Sharing

Programs like gain sharing are founded on the belief that, while managers are responsible for increasing productivity or reducing costs within their functions or departments, additional opportunities for these improvements exist in the hearts and minds of their employees. Further, these programs assume that to identify and experience these benefits, the company should establish a special reward system that links rewards to the gains the company receives.

Most managers agree that heightened employee participation, interest, involvement, and empowerment are necessary if a company is to maintain its competitiveness. The incentive for people to find more efficient methods, produce greater quality, or reduce costs has to be more than simply keeping their jobs. If employees are to be expected to generate these types of ideas and efforts, then they need to share the gains from their ideas and efforts. To expect managers to design, install, administer, and champion this type of crusade on their own, without any structured or top-down commitment, is expecting too much— especially if those managers aren't given any budget for the initial start-up phase.

Managers could walk around handing out fifty-dollar bills for any activity that the manager feels is helping to increase productivity or reduce costs, but this practice tends to reward the same people over and over, and only for activities that can be specifically measured on a small, focused scale. But how do you get everyone to turn off lights, not take supplies home, or reduce personal phone calls? How do you encourage people to suggest or make seemingly minor changes in placement of equipment and to apply improved methods or techniques to reduce scrap and rework? All of these activities result in small but cumulative productivity improvements and cost savings. This kind of continuous improvement program calls for some type of gain-sharing reward program.

A gain-sharing program typically establishes a benchmark number that represents the average for employee-influenced costs as a percentage of produced output at a specific period in time. If the program reflects a benchmark of 80 percent of the value of the output, then any improvement that results in the costs being a lower percentage than 80 percent is translated into dollars that become the distribution base.

Performance over the quarter, for example, is measured against that benchmark, and a portion of any savings, generally 50 percent, is distributed to the entire group of eligible employees. The other 50 percent is retained by the company. The benchmark remains the same for an appropriate length of time in order to promote the ongoing practice of the improved methods. The benchmark changes when the equipment, major processes, or products are changed.

Companies often want to use a targeted amount or performance goal as the benchmark instead of a historical average. When management sets a target, it is really telling employees that it assumes that there are inefficiencies within the operation that add up to the difference between the goal and reality. Many people see this as an accusation instead of an attempt at cooperation. Also, if the target is missed but the employees still record an improvement, management may have to grant an award anyway. The target may have been too aggressive and, in the employees' minds, not realistic for a given period of time. It's more effective to simply ask the employees to do as well as they can and then wait to see what develops.

Returning one-half of the savings to the employee group bothers many managers. They fail to realize that the savings would not be there in the first place were it not for the extra employee effort and the program that motivates it. This motivation can be established early on by including the employees in the design, installation, and administration of the gain-sharing program.

A gain-sharing committee of nonmanagement and management personnel should design the program over a period of time. During that time, committee members should solicit input from their peers. As they do, news of the concept will spread and interest will build. The committee should do everything, from developing the written program description to introducing the program to other employees and administering it once it is installed. This provides the company with in-house expertise that can be used to alter the program when changes are needed to correct oversights in the initial design or to accommodate changes in company equipment, operation, or product. Purchasing a program "off the shelf" will not provide this internal level of participation or ongoing involvement.

What determines the success of a gain-sharing program is a company's ability to measure its costs and other related aspects of the business. If a company does not have reliable measurement systems in place, it cannot conceivably install or benefit from a gain-sharing effort. But it probably doesn't matter, because if the company is not measuring its costs reliably, reducing them is not its top priority.

Skill-Based Pay

Skill-based pay started in manufacturing operations that use cellular production units. These units need employees who can perform a number of different jobs requiring different skills. Employees who learn a number of skills can earn additional rewards depending on the number of skills learned and how frequently they use them in the different jobs.

Skill-based pay works for operations that need flexible employees who can be assigned different jobs from one day to the next. It results from the reality that in most quickly changing manufacturing operations, jobs can seldom be narrowly structured or defined. Skill-based pay has also been applied successfully to other nonexempt job groups, such as the office clerical areas. Wherever jobs require a broad set of varying skills, this concept has possible application.

One of the key advantages of skill-based pay is that an employee is paid an ongoing higher rate of pay for a specific higher skill only if that skill is actually applied during a certain time frame. For example, an employee may earn a set base pay amount, plus two additional incremental skill-pay amounts representing the two additional skills he or she has mastered. As long as the employee works in jobs requiring those two skills during a thirty-day period, those additional two skill-pay amounts are paid to him or her. But if that employee is assigned to jobs requiring only one of the skills during that thirty-day period, the variable pay is just for one skill. Although this kind of compensation does require extra administration, it saves money because the pay for a skill that is not consistently utilized is not built into the employee's base pay.

But pay for new skills shouldn't be confused with increases in workload. For example, a secretary who is asked to perform work for an additional individual may feel that extra pay is justified for this extra work. But what the secretary is being asked to do does not involve any new skills; in fact, the duties are basically the same. Just because the workload allows additional time to be devoted to the second person does not necessarily warrant any additional pay other than overtime.

Using Nonpay Rewards

Every reward program costs the company something, but there are numerous nonpay rewards that do not change employees' taxable income. Many of these nonpay rewards are, in the minds of most people, perceived as recognition, not reward—a subtle but important distinction. A company also needs to reward its employees through recognition. If it doesn't include some of the following items in its reward structure, management and non-management employees alike will see it as not doing all it can to show that it appreciates its people.

- Immediate verbal or written praise
- Small lump-sum cash awards (grossed up to cover taxes)
- Recognition banquets—employee of the year, etc.
- Recognition posters—employee of the month, etc.
- Thanksgiving turkeys

- ❏ Gift certificates
- ❏ Improved office space, furnishings, equipment, etc.
- ❏ Club membership
- ❏ Discount certificates
- ❏ Trips
- ❏ Tickets to events
- ❏ Seniority awards
- ❏ Company goods, products, equipment, etc.
- ❏ Lunches, dinners, etc.
- ❏ Subscriptions to magazines, product-of-the-month clubs, etc.
- ❏ Charitable contributions in employee name

While these types of rewards may seem lightweight compared to the pay-based rewards most firms consider or administer, they have a definite place in the reward structure. But companies must keep two points in mind when they install nonpay rewards.

First, nonpay rewards cannot take the place of a fair and competitive pay-based reward system. Employees will not be fooled by an attempt to substitute nonpay rewards when pay is expected or more appropriate. Nonpay rewards do not protect or improve the lifestyle of the person receiving them, which is what people look for in return for their efforts or labors. These are no more than pats on the back.

No matter how liberal the pay-based reward system, there will always be some employees who feel that they and the company would be better served if the money being spent on nonpay rewards were put directly into their pay. This attitude can prevail if a company doesn't support nonpay rewards with a competitive take-home pay program. In that situation, a nonpay rewards system does more damage than good.

Second, management has to consider the consequences of discontinuing certain nonpay rewards. Rewards such as verbal and written praise should never be discontinued. Other items, such as Thanksgiving turkeys, may become burdens to the company as it grows. But unless you have ever tried to discontinue giving out these turkeys, you won't understand the degree to which people have become accustomed to the symbolism associated with this activity. Many companies attempt to buy out the gift by adjusting employee base pay in an amount thought to be equal to the discontinued reward.

The key point to keep in mind when considering these types of rewards is the purpose they are designed to serve. They are simply short-term thank-you notes directed at getting employees to continue some form of behavior. Like other reward programs, a nonpay reward program requires long-term sincerity and energy on the part of management if it is to be effective. Without commitment from management, nonpay rewards become just another time-consuming duty and expense.

Key Ingredients of Variable-Reward Programs: Time and Energy

When it comes to reward programs, managers can't give just cursory attention, make a quick call, and move on to other management concerns. It takes time and energy to develop, implement, and manage a successful variable-reward program. And the more time and energy a company chooses to spend on rewards, the greater the chance that specific types or applications of rewards will have a favorable effect on the company's success or goals.

If the management feels that the company's operation is such that the way people are paid is not important, they can simply hire at rates and grant increases in amounts that get and keep the key people. People who are readily available in the labor market will come and go through what is considered normal turnover.

But if the operation can benefit from the employment of people who work best when they are rewarded under programs that require attention, management will have to spend more than a casual amount of time on reward issues. That additional time is devoted mainly to the measurement needed to support the distribution of the dollars involved.

As this book has consistently stressed, certain business operations produce better results when they employ certain types of people. And certain types of people will perform to specific levels of output only if they are rewarded in the appropriate manner. It follows, then, that for any company to be more competitive than its competition, it will have to manage a well-thought-out reward structure. A company can either accept this and spend the time and energy on rewards, or ignore the issue and hope to make up the deficiency through luck or time and energy in other areas.

Most businesses are properly conservative in their application of untried practices. But variable-reward techniques are far from untried in the business world. They have a proven record in certain applications. The trick is to evaluate their potential and then move ahead with the program that will best meet the needs of your own organization.

CHAPTER 12

Administering a Reward Program

Designing, developing, and installing a reward system and program is hard work. The ongoing administration of a reward system also presents challenges to a manager's judgment. This chapter reviews some of those challenges and suggests strategies you can use to keep your compensation and reward system as flexible and effective as it can be.

Management Training: A Must for Any Reward System

The key to managing a base-pay or variable-reward program is the manager's understanding of the entire reward system. Without a firm grasp of the philosophy behind the reward initiative, you will not be able to use this initiative effectively as a tool to accomplish company objectives and goals. Instead, it will become just another administrative obstacle that you may try to circumvent as you perform your day-to-day responsibilities.

All managers should receive training in the critical elements of the organization's reward programs and policies. Because it is your responsibility to communicate and apply the entire range of company programs and policies, including the reward system, you need to understand the philosophy, objectives, and application of the reward system, and exceptions to it.

This training has two goals. First, it will enable you to confidently answer questions about the reward system. It is appropriate to refer questions about profit-sharing accounts or benefits administration problems to human resources. But telling employees to see someone else for an explanation of your reward system is tantamount to admitting that you don't fully understand your job.

The second goal of training is to ensure that the reward program is consistently managed throughout the company or function. Once a company decides that it needs or wants a certain type of reward procedure, it has to make sure that individual managers do not take it upon themselves to apply it in differing manners. Training will prevent this mismanagement, whether it is innocent or intentional.

Communicating the Program to Employees

Some companies keep their employees completely in the dark on everything besides base pay. Other organizations, such as unionized or government operations, publish everything about their pay policies and programs and make it available to anyone inside or outside of the organization. How much your employees should know about your company's reward policies and programs depends upon your organization.

I think any company that installs a reward program over and above its base-rate program should tell its employees about the program and its objectives. Consider a sales commission plan that, through its design, encourages the sales staff to sell more of some products than others. How effective would that plan be if it weren't communicated to employees? The same is true of any variable-pay program. In order to be motivated by a program, people need to understand how it works and why it works the way it does.

The range maximums of base-pay systems should also be communicated. Full disclosure is the only way managers can prepare employees whose pay levels are approaching the top of their respective ranges. Those people need to be aware that their earnings will be limited unless they learn additional, higher-level skills. Whether they can reasonably expect a promotion or will receive minimal pay adjustments for some time needs to be openly discussed. If range maximums have been communicated, you don't have to worry about how to break the news to the employee. You can concern yourself with explaining why there are range maximums—and if you've been through training, then you know the answer.

The most common and traditional way to communicate a reward program and policy is through an employee manual that outlines its purpose and procedures. Unfortunately, most employees lose interest on the second page of a thick manual. A question-and-answer format will do a better job of getting and keeping the employee's attention. If the questions chosen are the ones in which the employees are most interested, and the answers are complete and open, such a series of questions and answers can effectively convey the key points of the program.

Communicating reward policies must be an ongoing practice. To announce and explain a compensation program at its introduction but never mention it again will accomplish little. Turnover can result in employees who have never heard anything about the reward program, especially if your company lacks a thorough new-hire orientation program. Don't make communication a one-time event. Make it an ongoing part of your management duties.

Administering the Program

Any organization that is growing or changing with its industry will have to adapt its reward system to changes in job content. Such changes may require current employees to learn new equipment or skills, or may mean that the company must add people with different skills or from different professions while dealing with current employees whose skills can't quite meet the company's changing situation.

It's difficult for a reward program to anticipate, plan for, and accommodate these changes. Adjusting the internal reward policy to accommodate new demands during ongoing change is also a challenge for managers. But that's why it's called *manag-*

ing; if it only involved the same thing day after day, it would be called maintaining!

Many managers work hard to stay within payroll budget limits set for the department or function. But because these parameters are driven and controlled by the marketplace and the organization's performance needs, chances are you just have to live with the cost of labor as expressed in the marketplace. Therefore, most of the pay and reward problems you will deal with will involve one of these four issues:

1. Short- and long-term changes in job content or performance requirements
2. Staffing or training needs dictated by those changing requirements
3. Meeting the reward expectations of employees involved in the changes
4. Establishing or maintaining the internal equity and external competitiveness of reward levels

The first issue is one that every manager faces as the responsibilities of her or his employees change. Over time, managers tend to change the daily responsibilities of some or all employees under them by adding or removing various duties. This gradual change in skills or accountabilities needs to be reviewed in terms of potential pay-level shifts in order to prevent employees from feeling resentful and the company from paying too much or too little for the actual jobs being performed.

The first three issues involve adapting to "change" and "expectations," both of which are unknowns. The fourth deals with the outcome of those unknowns—internal organizational needs and external market developments—and thus is also unknown. Because the company does not know the future in which it will have to operate, it should not attempt to install any type of reward structure that requires too much work to maintain, is too restrictive to management, or tries to anticipate what things will look like three or four years down the road.

Sadly, many companies do install a somewhat rigid structure that is designed to give management guidelines and direction, control costs, and last for several years. None of these reflect the reality that the organization will continue to change. When the reward structure becomes too binding, it becomes part of the problem. Managers now have to react to reward issues in a manner that stays within the program structure. The obvious alternative is to design a less restricting, more adaptable set of guidelines for managing reward problems.

The only companies that can afford to develop narrow pay ranges and tight increase guidelines are industry leaders that are so prominent that they can dictate pay structures and ranges. Everyone else needs to build a structure that gives room for managers to "wiggle" by providing ways to get around the structure.

A flexible rewards program facilitates the selection process; an antiquated, rigid system inhibits it. You may have very little time in which to make an offer to and hire desired or needed candidates or to develop a counteroffer to an employee who is threatening to leave. Requiring a manager like you to convince others, who may not understand the complete situation, of the need to react outside of the structure defeats the purpose of giving you the responsibility to achieve certain objectives, within specified time frames, in the first place.

The best approach is to create just enough of a framework to remind the manager that there is a general right and wrong way to operate. The wrong way is to do whatever you want to do or to react with whatever first comes to mind. The right way is to give some consideration to the ramifications that any decision will have for the company, the department, the employee concerned, and other employees. If your tactic survives this analysis, it just might be the right thing to do.

Evaluating Pay and Creating Pay Ranges

When pay ranges and job classifications have not been carefully established, pay for some jobs may be excessive relative to the external market, while pay ranges for others may overlap. To prevent wage compression and other problems, you need to group similar jobs together to ensure internal equity and provide the foundation for determining pay levels for newly created or changed jobs.

While not as scientific as some techniques used by compensation professionals, the techniques of ranking and broadbanding can help a manager or company group jobs into sets of jobs with similar skills or responsibilities and assign a pay range to each set, thus giving the organization a realistic and workable reward structure. Ranking is a means of evaluating jobs on the basis of their internal relationships. Broadbanding is a technique for grouping similar jobs together so that pay ranges can be established for each of the groups, based on the external market pay levels for some or all of the benchmark jobs. Both of these techniques are suitable for setting up a first-time pay program or for evaluating changes in job content or staffing needs.

The ranking and broadbanding process evaluates job content, required skills, and assigned responsibilities, not people or their performance. This is an especially difficult discipline for managers who are guilty of creating jobs based on the capabilities or limitations of the individuals rather than creating jobs needed by the company and filling them with qualified people.

Ranking simply lists jobs in order of their impact on the company's overall goals and objectives on the basis of the responsibilities and skills assigned—that is, in order of their importance to the organization. The ranking exercise can be conducted by a committee of managers, the chief executive, or someone with a thorough knowledge of the jobs being ranked. Start by listing the top job and the least important job. Then follow up by pinpointing the second most important job and the second least important job, and so forth. The middle will be the toughest group to rank and will take the most time, especially if the exercise is being done by a committee and there is disagreement among the members.

Critics of this approach claim that it is too subjective and not quantitative in its method. They may recommend use of a more elaborate job evaluation system that requires the evaluation of job elements first. For each job, the values assigned to those elements are added, and the total is compared to the totals for other jobs as a means of determining the relationship between jobs. In reality, the subjectivity is still there; it is just buried in the elements of the job. All job evaluation is subjective.

The broadbanding process begins when the entire collection of jobs has been ranked. Broadbanding consists of grouping jobs with similar responsibilities and importance. The objective is to end up with groups of ten or twelve jobs. Thus, if an organization has sixty jobs, it should have five or six groups or bands of jobs.

Start at the top of the ranked list and compare each job to the one ranked above it and the one ranked below it. If the job is more similar to the one above it than to the one below, keep them together and go on to the next job on the list. When a job matches the one below more closely than it matches the one above, that job becomes the first job in the next band of jobs. For example, when comparing a vice president of operations up to the vice president of finance or down to the manager of purchasing, the match is to the job above. When the manager of purchasing is compared to vice president of operations and the job below, manager of assembly, the match is to the job below. Thus the manager of purchasing becomes the first job in the next band of jobs.

After the bands have been developed, you can establish a pay minimum and maximum for each one. Use some or all of the benchmark jobs and any available market salary survey information to set range maximums for the respective bands. If salary surveys are not available for all of the bands, extrapolate from those that are available to other bands. Generally there should be 25 to 30 percent difference from one band maximum to the next. Band minimums are not as critical.

A practical approach is to adhere to a policy of granting a 10 percent promotional pay increase to any employee whose responsibilities change enough to justify his or her moving into the next or any higher band. Salaries for new hires can be determined by matching the new hire with the experience of people in similar jobs within the appropriate band.

Adjusting Pay Ranges and Administering Pay Increases

The wage market is seldom static. Wages move up and down with supply and demand, movement of people into lateral jobs at other companies with accompanying wage increases, and union contract settlements. It is good policy to review this movement annually, with an eye toward possibly moving the company ranges in response to outside movements.

Let employees know that your policy is to review the market annually. Don't imply that the ranges will be adjusted annually; make it clear that they will be adjusted only when and if management feels it is appropriate. Not moving the ranges when necessary can cause employees to top out in their ranges and eventually to look outside the company for more money for the same job. It also has an impact if new hires are brought in at pay levels that create pressure on longer-service employees. These problems may arise even when you do move range maximums, but they will not be due to poor management of the reward structure.

The decision to move ranges upward should not be driven by the desire to create room for increases because current wages are pushing the maximums. The ranges should reflect the market and act as a lid on increases. You cannot make the field wider just because players are running out of bounds.

General Increases

General increases are across-the-board wage increases, generally limited to nonexempt employee groups. While they can take the place of a merit review pay increase program because they grant everyone in the employee group the same amount of increase on the same date, they can also cause problems with company pay ranges.

One company's merit pay program was designed to adjust pay range maximums upward whenever the market dictated it, with no accompanying general increase to the employees. The employees were, in effect, losing ground within their ranges whenever an adjustment took place. Eventually employees objected that they could never reach the maximums of their respective ranges. Because this was true, management developed a reward program that granted general increases equaling the amount of the range adjustment. Now the employees could maintain their positions within their ranges and also reach the maximums through merit increases.

But after a period of time, employees objected again, this time because there was no place to go once they reached the maximums of their ranges. A "what have you done for me lately?" attitude set in. As a result, management may go back to the system without general increases because the best performers—the ones who actually reach the top of their ranges through higher-than-average increases—are the most unhappy.

The problems facing this company stem from a lack of understanding of why the ranges were moved and general increases were granted. As a result, the company is having trouble communicating its reasoning to the employees. To prevent this, make it clear that pay range maximums are administrative controls and not necessarily a goal that every employee will reach.

Pay range maximums should be adjusted in anticipation of the market's movement over the upcoming year or so. The adjustment indicates where rewards should be in the future. Adjusting ranges to catch up with the market means that the company is at a disadvantage in terms of getting and keeping people. You should communicate this movement in anticipation of the market to employees, or they may think that they are presently underpaid relative to that market.

If you take this approach, you need not even consider a general increase, unless that is the only way in which employees receive pay increases. When the reward program is based on merit increases, range movement should be explained as providing room for future movement for high-performing employees. Make it clear that the maximums represent not where the market currently is, but where management expects the market to eventually be.

COLA Increases

COLA, or a cost-of-living-related pay adjustment, is a term that is often misused. COLA has very little to do with the actual economic forces that drive the wage market, although COLA increases do apply some pressure on those wages. Managers who use the term to identify any type of general increase simply do not understand the potential misunderstanding that they may be creating in the minds of the employees.

COLA is designed to maintain the employee's standard of living, which has little to do with the supply and demand for labor. The last thing any company should want is to get into the trap of protecting the standards of living that people have become accustomed to. This is the same as agreeing to purchase necessary resources from a supplier at a noncompetitive cost just to help that supplier to stay in business.

Inflation that becomes a factor in the cost of living will eventually show up in wage movement in the marketplace. That's when it's time to react—but then only to that wage market. To tell employees that the company is granting a COLA communicates the wrong message.

Promotion Rewards

Because nobody really knows how an employee will perform in the job he or she is promoted into, some managers are reluctant to give any reward or increase at the time of the promotion. These managers would rather wait three to six months to see just how the employee performs. You can imagine how the newly promoted person feels, knowing that not only does the boss lack confidence in him or her, but the new job will feature more responsibilities without additional pay. In my view, employees who receive promotions should always be given a promotion increase based on their performance track record because they will be doing more in the new job than they were doing before. It's as simple as that!

Another problem with promotion rewards has to do with the percentage difference from one pay range to the next. If that difference is less than 25 to 30 percent, an employee getting a reasonable promotion increase of 10 percent will have a pay rate that is too high in the new band or range. There may not be enough room for that person to receive subsequent pay increases for more than a year or two.

There should always be enough of a jump from range maximum to range maximum to allow an employee who is at the top of a range and who receives a fair promotional increase to end up in the lower half of the new range. The manager who does not ensure that the reward structure is designed in this manner may find that recently promoted individuals are bumping against their maximums almost as soon as they begin to be accomplished in their jobs. That's not a good time for you to be telling them that they cannot receive appropriate rewards for their performance!

Using Exceptional Rewards

Exceptional rewards are exceptions to a pay structure that allow you to reward an outstanding performer without changing formal policy. This kind of latitude lets you retain a vice president of sales who is constantly being offered opportunities by the competition, or reward an engineer at the top of his salary range who is not interested in management but whose patents built the company.

In order to offer exceptional rewards fairly, you must be very clear about the means and goals of your company's reward program. Such an understanding will help you limit these exceptional rewards to people whose performance is unique or very far above the norm, instead of making everyone an exception.

Red-Circle Reward Levels

In the lexicon of the compensation professional, a "red-circle rate" is a rate paid to an employee that is above the maximum for his or her pay range.

Companies allow red-circle rates for two reasons. First, sometimes the market for a specific job is just not in line with that for jobs with similar content, and the only way to select or retain someone is to bend the rules a little. You don't want to distract a high-performing employee by refusing him or her an increase just because your range maximum doesn't fit the market for this one position. It's better to exempt it from the normal administrative controls by referring to it as a red-circle rate.

The second reason is that without this exception, managers

may be tempted to inflate job responsibilities in order to create a promotion where one otherwise would not exist, or to push for a job to be upgraded into the next higher band or range on the basis that more duties have been added. Both of these situations can distort internal equity—the relationship between jobs in your company. When an employee has topped out in the range but there are good business reasons for granting an increase, this red-circle provision can accommodate the situation without forcing the manager to distort the reward system.

However, proposed red-circle rates must be rigidly reviewed and controlled in order to avoid violating the consistent administration of wage costs.

Lump-Sum Rewards

Lump-sum rewards offer another way to deal with solid performers who have reached the maximum of their pay range but deserve some form of reward. Instead of granting an increase in their base pay—thereby placing their pay level above the normal market or company rate for that job—determine the percentage reward they would normally receive and issue a one-time payment equaling the annualized amount of that percentage of their base pay. The lump-sum approach honors the prevailing system of controlling payroll costs but allows a year of good performance to be rewarded without permanently influencing base-pay levels.

The employee's performance record should indicate that a lump-sum merit reward was issued. After a year or two of lump-sum rewards, the range adjustments generally provide enough room to again grant a base-pay increase.

Exempt Overtime

Excessive overtime has always been a cause of pay compression between nonexempt employees and their exempt managers, because it has a real impact on annual earnings.

The Fair Labor Standards Act allows most employers to get by without paying overtime to supervisory and management personnel. Companies that take strict advantage of this often find nonexempt employees earning more than their bosses, leaving bosses to wonder why they ever left the rank and file for management. But when overtime is almost a way of life at a company, it will often pay some form of overtime to affected management personnel.

Policies calling for straight time after the first five hours of overtime to first-level supervisors and managers are examples of one approach. This avoids paying for casual overtime or shift overlap, such as time spent getting the department started in the morning and closing or turning over the department to the next shift at night. It pays only for scheduled overtime that has been approved.

But excessive overtime can still be a problem if the base-pay spread between nonexempt and exempt manager is not great enough. An alternative in this situation is to pay straight time from hour one for all scheduled overtime. This at least extends the crossover on the earnings curve.

Many companies that employ exempt professionals such as engineers, accountants, and buyers are faced with periods of extended overtime for those personnel. Management has four options for dealing with this issue: hiring more permanent staff, contracting for temporary people, paying some form of straight-time premium in place of overtime to the affected employees, or ignoring the issue. Temporary staffing will avoid the cost of adding full-time people, although bringing temps up to speed can take time if the work is unique to the company. Ignoring the problem has many obvious drawbacks. That leaves the payment of some form of premium to current exempt people. If they can continue to handle the workload, this is the preferable course in most cases.

Afterword: Go Forth and Manage!

The most difficult problem facing every business is the need for effective managers and effective management practices. Good products and services will flounder in the market if management is marginal; marginal products and services may succeed if management is good. Likewise, state-of-the-art equipment, centralized locations, overindulgent reward and benefit programs, or just-in-time inventory systems cannot compensate for the manager who is afraid to deal with shipping department personnel who are continually high on their favorite mind- or mood-altering substance. Sooner or later, mislabeled goods, damaged goods, delayed goods, or stolen goods will displace every other aspect of the operation and become the major problem.

In order to succeed, every business has to be able to answer yes to two simple questions:

1. Are we selling enough of our product or service?
2. Are we selling at the right price to make our necessary profit?

The first question has to do with having a presence in the market. But presence is not enough; even Packard, Tucker, and Edsel had a presence in the automotive market. The second question has to do with effectiveness in managing costs, resources, and pricing. Ford, Chevy, and Honda are effective. If the answer to both of those questions is yes, the company can probably stay in business for a while.

The same two questions determine how a manager is performing. If a manager is simply maintaining a presence, he or she is not doing much to ensure his or her longevity. If, on the other hand, that manager is also effective in managing responsibilities, he or she has a valuable skill on which to build a career. What *effective* means is not difficult to determine. The following guidelines identify the characteristics of effectiveness in managers at every level, be they supervisors, managers, superintendents, or vice presidents:

1. Knowing and understanding the key short- and long-term objectives of the company, the department, and the jobs in that department
2. Working toward those objectives at all times, not allowing distractions or activity to take the place of accomplishment
3. Translating and transferring objectives to subordinates and ensuring the successful accomplishment of those objectives through the:
   □ *Selection* of employees who have the necessary attitudes, skills, and energy to perform the specific jobs required
   □ *Direction* of employees through clear, concise, and frequent outlining of required activities
   □ *Evaluation* of employees against scheduled events and dates that ensure accomplishment of the key objectives
   □ *Reward* of employees that is appropriate to the level of accomplishment, not efforts
4. Reacting quickly to any signs that progress toward objectives is being hampered by any aspect within the responsibilities of their job

Many managers who fail to perform up to their full potential lack self-confidence. Not trusting one's judgment of what needs to be done in certain situations is the dilemma faced by many people new to the ranks of management. That lack of confidence generally stems from two concerns: not being sure that something is really wrong, and not being sure what steps or action to take to deal with the situation.

The first concern involves instinct and experience. If your senses tell you that something needs attention, you are most likely right. Remember, there is a reason why you were put in a position of responsibility: Some more seasoned manager felt that you had the necessary tools. All you have to do is trust in yourself.

The second concern, not being sure what steps or action to take, also involves instinct and experience. In this case, you gain the experience through practice, practice, and more practice. The more you deal with management situations, the more confident you become.

Some people believe that it's better to do nothing than to do something that might turn out to be wrong. What a cowardly way to manage a career! The odds are that whatever you try will not be far from the best that could have been done. Companies suffer more from missed or lost opportunities than they do from things that were done but could have been done better. These things will be done better the next time, but only because they were tried the first time. It is little victories on top of little victories that have impact, not putting off challenges, hoping that they will go away. Floodwaters go away, but they leave a real mess behind them. It's better to resist them at the proper time in the proper places.

Managers have to learn to live with and learn from their mistakes. This is not the same as overlooking or avoiding them. Good managers seldom simply accept situations. They always try to make things better or find the real problem. Reputations are often made on no more than being the person who is always willing to step up and face the problem. That, in itself, creates self-confidence. It also causes others to have confidence in you, because most people know that the guy who cuts in is usually a pretty good dancer. Managers need to have the courage to identify, accept, and affect reality.

The critical element in a manager's environment is the people around and above him or her. Sometimes the manager seems to be trapped in a pattern of kicking butt and kissing butt—pounding on the people reporting to you, and bending over backward for the people that you report to. That's because rewards come mainly from the people above, not the people below. While it's nice to have a team of loyal employees reporting to you, that loyalty is often created at the expense of effectiveness. A manager needs respect more than loyalty. Respect is based on continually doing the right things, in the right way, for the right reasons. These actions also bring respect from the people the manager reports to.

A manager can be a hero to both groups only if he or she is effective. Effectiveness is related to the depth a manager develops while practicing these four management elements. All managers practice these elements some of the time. But the more consistently you select, direct, evaluate, and reward, the more depth you will gain. In the last analysis, it is this depth that determines your effectiveness as a manager. The more depth you develop, the more impact you will have on your organization and your career.

Go forth and manage, as you select, direct, evaluate, and reward!

Index

accomplishment, 52
accountability, 103
action orientation, 141
action steps
    assignment of, 66, 73–74, 74–81
    with deadlines, 68–69
    determining, 102
    in evaluation, 122–123
    objectives in, 66
    performing, 92–96
    substeps of, 69–74, 78, 79
action words, for job, 6
ad copy, 22–23, 44
administration
    of pay increases, 189–193
    of reward program, 185–187
advertising
    on Internet, 24
    newspaper, 22–23
    radio and cable TV, 25–26
    word-of-mouth, 26
alumni associations, 25
ambush-style direction, 93
annual review, job, 81–82
Apollo moon mission, 3–4, 171
appearance, 28
association newsletters, 25
attitude, 28–29, 33
    "can do," 50
    problems with, 107
    rewards from, 152

automatic pay progression, 160–
    161, 163
    advantages and disadvantages
        of, 161
    evaluation with, 164
    pay grade ranges with, 164–165
    withholding rewards in, 165
autonomy, 116

base-pay systems, 156–160,
    160–161
    range maximums of, 184–185
behavioral issues, 106–108
benchmark, employee-influenced
    cost, 177
benchmark jobs, 159
bonus program, 171, 173–174
borderline performers, 143–145
brainstorming, 90
broadbanding, 188–189
business intelligence, 21
business plan, 59–60

candidate-job matching, 7
candidates
    checking references of, 40–41
    employed vs. unemployed,
        18–20
    failure to find, 44
    ideal profile for, 16–17
    interesting in position, 20–26

candidates (*continued*)
　internal vs. external, 17–18
　interview of, 32–40
　locating, 17–20
　making job offer to, 41–43
　must-have qualities in, 16–17
　qualified, 15–27
　relocation of, 19
　screening of, 29–30
"can do" attitude, 50
career development, 65
change, 50, 54–55
COLA pay increases, 191–192
commissions, sales, 175–176
communication
　assessing skills for, 37
　of responsibilities, action steps,
　　and objectives, 102
　of reward program, 184–185
company
　capabilities of, 57
　culture of, 17, 50
　developing goals of, 67
compensation
　base-pay system of, 156–160
　evaluation and, 123–124
　issues of, 28
　vs. rewards, 151–152
　see also pay; rewards; salary
competition
　accurate assessment of, 57
　job candidates from, 21–22
completion, sense of, 142
confidence, 127–129
confrontation, 126–127
consistency, 10–11, 51, 147–148
control, limits of, 142
corrective action, progress of, 146
costs, focus on, 154–156
creativity, 10–11
critical incidents file, 108, 122
customer satisfaction, 170–172

deadlines, 51–52
　action steps with, 68–74
　cushion in, 80

decisiveness, 131–132
delivery time, 12
department progress, 97–98
direction, 45, 49–52
　ambush-style, 93
　areas for, 56–59
　basics of, 77–81
　clarity of, 50–52, 63
　determining, 47–61
　in evaluation, 102–103
　job audit and, 81–82
　overload of, 55
　purpose of, 64, 85
　reasons managers don't give
　　proper, 52–55
　skills needed for, 78–81
　strategic plan–based, 45
　time spent on, 1
　too much, 55–56
　in top-down management,
　　59–61
　training management in, 62–84
direction expertise training, 64
disagreement, 126–127
discretionary reward method, 174
discrimination, 105–106
Drucker, Peter, on reality, 58

80/20 rule, 108
employed candidates, 18–20
employee self-evaluation form,
　113–114, 121
employees
　accommodating, 135–137
　improving use of, 132–133
　independent, 104
　pay progression programs for,
　　160–161
　replacement of, 8
　training of, 85–98
energy, in variable-reward pro-
　gram, 181–182
energy force, 85
energy reserves, 56

equity, internal, 158–159, 186, 187–188
evaluation, 50, 99–100
  confidence in, 127–129
  employee-driven, 108–116
  forms for, 111–114, 115
  how not to use, 135–137
  how to use, 134–135
  management review board in, 147–148
  managers and, 116–117
  off-the-shelf vs. customized, 109
  performance categories in, 137–147
  selecting format for, 109–110
  what to include in, 101–117
  of when things get done, 101
  see also performance evaluation
evaluation meeting, 118
  confidence in, 127–129
  input data for, 121–127
  personnel use and, 132–133
  productive, 129–132
  reasons for hating, 118–120
  unfocused, 105–106
exceptional rewards, 193–195
exempt jobs, 13, 159
  merit rewards for, 160–161
  overtime in, 194–195
expectations
  employees who exceed, 138
  employees who fall below, 139
  employees who meet, 138–139
  performance, 137–138
  unrealistic, 105
expertise, creation of, 64
external candidates, 17–18

face-to-face interview, 32–34
  evaluating attitude in, 33
  intuition in, 38–39
  listening in, 36–38
  methods in, 39–40
  sticking to outline in, 35–36
  structuring of, 34–35
  time use in, 36
Fair Labor Standards Act, 159, 194–195
feedback
  on job responsibilities, 6
  from lost candidates, 44
flexible organization, 93–94
function, progress measurement of, 97
functional responsibility, 70–74

gain sharing, 171, 176–178
gatekeeper, in evaluation review, 148
goals
  ceilings and minimums for, 84
  focus on, 64–65
  translation of, 66
  see also company objectives; objectives
goal-setting process, 54–55
"group grope" technique, 40
group rewards, 169–170

hiring
  vs. filling jobs, 1
  lateral vs. promotion, 157

ideal-candidate profile, 16–17
ideas
  asking employees for, 88
  encouraging of, 90
individual rewards, 169–170
inflation, 192
input data collection, 121–127
internal candidates, 17–18
internal customer evaluation form, 115
internal growth issues, 60
interview
  face-to-face, 32–40
  telephone, 30–32

intuition, 38–39
involvement, high-level, 87–88

job audit, 7–9
  direction and, 81–82
  job description in, 11
job description
  agreement on, 12
  around individual, 135–137
  changes in, 9
  clear, 78
  drafting of, 9–12
  flexible vs. rigid, 93–94
  in performance evaluation, 123
  purposes of, 9–11
  review and revision of, 81–82
  sample of with objectives, 79
job offer, 41–43
job responsibilities
  action words for writing, 6
  benefits of defining, 7
  determining, 4–7
  list of, 5
job tasks, 1
  annual review of, 81–82
  defining components of, 92–93
  ranking of, 4–6
job-related references, 40–41
jobs
  categories of, 13
  definition of, 3–14
  filling, 1, 28–44
  price range for, 157–159
  spreading word about, 20–26
  steps in defining, 4
  urgency of, 12

knowledge, 56
  translating into action, 64

lateral hiring, 157
leadership, sign of, 64–65
limitations, overcoming, 64
listening, 36–38

loyalty, 151
  building of, 51
lump-sum rewards, 194

management
  bonuses for, 173–174
  good, 64–65
  positions in, 13
  top-down, 59–61
  training of, 62–84, 75, 76,
    183–184
management promotion, 141–143
management review board,
    147–148
management skills, 125–126
managers
  assigning action steps, 74–81
  attitudes of toward evaluation,
    118–120
  effective, 198–200
  evaluation of, 125–126, 198
  evaluation skill of, 117
  first-level, 96–97
  as independent contractors, 71
  internal customers of, 71–72
  need for effective, 197
  people around, 199–200
  "report card" for, 116–117
  responsibilities of, 53
  training of, 66–81
  traits of successful, 141–143
measurement, 57–59
  of nonmanagement personnel
    training, 97–98
  of performance, 103–106
membership lists, 25
mental toughness, 142
merit rewards
  advantages and disadvantages
    of, 161
  evaluation with, 163–164
  pay grade ranges with, 164–165
  pay increases in, 160–161
  withholding of, 165–166

methods, vs. results, 56
mistakes, learning from, 199

networking, 26
nonexempt employees, 13, 159
    overtime for, 194–195
nonpay rewards, 179–181
not retainable performance cate-
    gory, 139, 146–147

objectives
    ability to prioritize, 142
    annual review of, 81–82
    areas for setting, 48
    assigning to employees, 80
    ceilings/minimums for, 83–84
    company-level, 59
    departmental, 60, 66
    directing employees toward, 53
    in evaluation, 122–123
    as everyone's job, 80–81
    failure to communicate, 58–59
    focusing on, 58
    functional, 59, 66
    individual-level, 60
    interrelated, 71
    in interview, 34–35
    in job description, 79
    local, 83
    sharing with employees, 90
    status report on, 81
    of strategic plan, 47–48
    translation of, 48–49, 66, 67, 68–
        74, 80, 90, 198
    understanding of, 198
    working from, 94
    working toward, 198
    see also goals
occupations, reasons for choosing,
    28
Odiorne, George, 30 percent gap
    theory of, 58–59
offer letter, 43
outplacement firms, 26

oversight, 53
overtime, exempt, 194–195
ownership, sense of, 142

Patton, 52
pay
    evaluation of, 187–189
    grade ranges of, 164–165
    maximums for, 184–185
    ranges of, 156–159, 187–193
    rigid structure of, 186–187
    skill-based, 178–179
    see also compensation; rewards;
        salary
pay increases
    administration of, 189–193
    annual, 157
    COLA, 191–192
    false, 136
    general, 190–191
    merit vs. automatic, 160–161
    with promotion, 192–193
peer review, 110–116
perception, 56–57
performance
    of borderline performers, 144
    categories of, 137–148
    compensation based on,
        151–152
    measurement of, 103–106
    rewards for, 153–154, 163,
        169–170
    standards of, 12
    steps to improve, 120–133
performance evaluation, 118,
    127–129
    benefits of, 117
    categories in, 137–148
    consistency in, 147–148
    forms for, 123
    guidelines for, 127–128
    how not to use, 135–137
    how to use, 134–135
    importance of, 103–106

performance evaluation
(*continued*)
management input in, 125–126
in merit vs. automatic progression programs, 164
passing judgment in, 119–120
preparation for, 121–122
principles of, 102
productive vs. destructive,
101–102
purposes of, 134–135
steps in, 102–103
surprises in, 118–119
too brief, 120
performance evaluation meeting
confidence in, 127–129
confrontation in, 126–127
decisiveness in, 131–132
employee comparisons in, 131
highlighting significance in, 131
instruction sheet to prepare employees for, 125
manager's guide for, 130–132
open discussion in, 130
preparation for, 124–125
productive, 129–132
specifics in, 130–131
termination process in, 147
personal reference, 40
personality differences, 51
personality issues, 38–39
personnel utilization, improving,
132–133
piecework, 171
placement fees, 23–24
policy violation, 107
poor performance, 106–107
possible-retention performance
category, 139, 145–146
preemployment testing, 38
probing interview style, 33
process
commitment to, 142
goals and, 54–55

productive time, focus on,
154–156
professional associations, 23–24
profit sharing, companywide, 171
progress
continuous monitoring of, 80
measurement of, 97–98
progress reports, 53
progress review, 102
progressive discipline forms, 107
promotion
false, 136–137
pay increases with, 192–193
promotion potential
immediate or eventual, 138,
139–141
management position, 141–143
questionable, 139, 143–145
publications, trade and professional, 23–24

qualifications, 28
quality, rewards for, 170–172
question-and-answers, 90–92

ranking, 188
"reach-in" process, 21–22
reality
defining, 57
measurement of, 57–59
vs. perception, 56–57
red-circle reward level, 193–194
reference checking, 40–41
relocation issues, 19
responsibilities
determining core set of, 102
of managers, 53
translating objectives into,
48–49
results
clearly defining, 45
evaluation based on, 103–104
management skills and, 126

vs. methods, 56
rewards for, 149
résumé database, 23
résumé search services, 24
résumés, 29–30
retainer arrangement, 23–24
rewards, 149
　administering of, 185–187
　base pay as, 156–160
　communicating to employees,
　　184–185
　definition of, 151
　exceptional, 193–195
　management training for,
　　183–184
　merit vs. automatic, 160–161,
　　163
　nonpay, 179–181
　as part of selection, 152–154
　purpose of, 151–166
　time and cost for, 154–156
　variable, 167–182
　withholding of, 165–166
　see also compensation; pay;
　　salary
rigid organization, 94

salary
　ceilings on, 157–159
　in job advertisment, 23
　maximums for, 158–159
　in offer letter, 43
　range for, 11, 13–14, 156–158
　see also compensation; pay
sales commission programs, 171
salespeople, commissions to,
　175–176
school bulletin boards, 25
scientific management, 49–50
screening, 29–30
search process, 15
search/employment firms, 23–24
selection, 1
　defining job in, 4–14
　rewards as part of, 152–154

self-confidence, lack of, 198–199
Sheriff-and-Posse Strategy,
　104–106
skill-based pay, 178–179
skilled trades, pay for, 160–161
Stanford-Binet test, 38
status report, 81
strategic business objectives, 80
strategic plan, 45, 47, 66
　implementation of, 75–76,
　　95–96
　for nonmanagement program,
　　95–96
　objectives of, 47–48
　presentation of, 66
　rationale behind, 89
　sharing with employees, 89–92
　specific responsibilities in,
　　48–49
stress interview, 39–40
structure
　vs. creativity, 10–11
　importance of, 10
successful business, keys to,
　197–198
successful management, elements
　of, 1
supervision, 80/20 rule in, 108
supervisor evaluation form,
　111–112
suspensions, 107
Syrus, Publilius, on standards, 104

Taylor, Frederick, on scientific
　management, 49–50
teamwork, 51
telephone interview, 30–32
temporary employment agencies,
　26
termination process, 147
testing services, 38
30 percent gap, 58–59
3-by-5 card test, 37

time
  focus on, 154–156
  in variable-reward program,
    181–182
top-down management, 59–61
trade associations, 23–24
training
  in assigning action steps, 74–81
  in direction, 62–84
  explaining need for, 86
  finding positive name for, 65
  goal of, 64
  importance of, 62–63
  management, 183–184
  necessity of, 63–66
  of nonmanagement personnel,
    85–98
  phases of, 66–81
training program, 96–97
  annual, 63
  home-grown, 65–66
  measuring progress of, 97–98
  nonmanagement, phases of,
    89–96
  participants in, 67–68
  positioning of, 86–89
  purpose of, 64
  question-and-answer session
    on, 90–92

reasons for participating in,
    86–87
trust, 127

understanding, of evaluation,
    127–128
unions, 160–161
unproductive time, 154–156

value systems, 172–173
variable-reward programs
  definition of, 167–168
  for groups or individuals,
    169–170
  to increase quality, 170–172
  key ingredients of, 181–182
  questions to ask about, 172
  selecting and installing, 172–179
  why managers don't like,
    168–169

wage freezes, 165–166
wage market fluctuations,
    189–190
Wall Street Journal, weekly em-
    ployment issue of, 30
Wonderlic, 38
work flowchart, 8
workforce, clear direction of,
    50–51
work-related drive, evaluating, 33